Etheric Materialization Into Form!

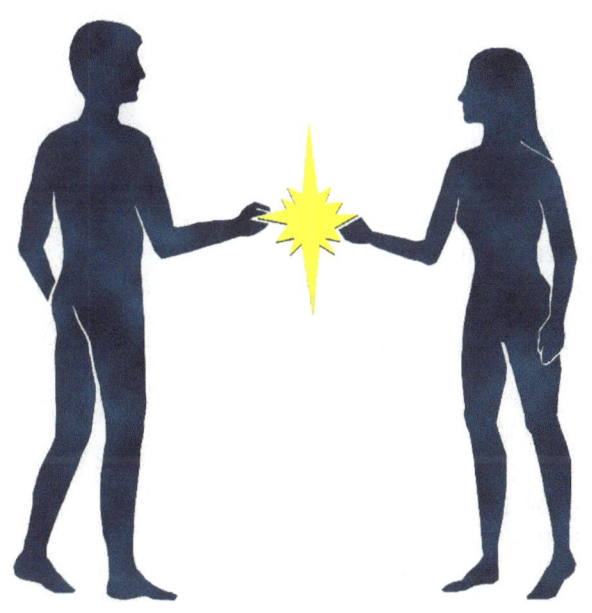

Christopher Alan Anderson

Etheric Materialization Into Form
Copyright ©2025 Christopher Alan Anderson

ISBN 978-1506-915-15-9 PBK
ISBN 978-1506-915-16-6 EBK

July 2025

Published and Distributed by
First Edition Design Publishing, Inc.
P.O. Box 17646, Sarasota, FL 34276-3217
www.firsteditiondesignpublishing.com

ALL RIGHTS RESERVED. No part of this book publication may be reproduced, stored in a retrieval system, or transmitted in any form or by any means — electronic, mechanical, photocopy, recording, or any other — except brief quotation in reviews, without the prior permission of the author or publisher.

www.manandwomanbalance.com

Preface

To you the reader:

Enclosed is a writing that came to me one night when I was half asleep. Actually, it surprised me. I, like so many others, have been searching for a way to manifest my desires. Will what you read herein work for you? I don't know; I think it can. Let me just say, if you make this writing your own than I will say YES, it can work for you.

Perhaps the most difficult part here is an understanding of terms. For example, the word *etheric*, what does that term mean? Does it have something to do with the ether? And didn't science prove long ago there is no such thing as an ether? How about the word *light?* Wow, there is a term that has multiple meanings. So, a good part of this treatise is to get a familiarity of terms, at least as I am using them.

Also, I use a number to quotes, some from my earlier writings and some from other authors. I think they help in clarifying things. For titles that are from other authors, I list the author and the title. For titles from my own writings, I just list the title. So, if you see a quote that does not have an author listed you can assume the author is me.

I hope you will give some time and thought to this writing. We are living in very uncertain times. Navigating through these times is not easy. I am only here to open a door; it is up to you to walk through it.

Christopher Alan Anderson
January 24, 2025

P.S. To Giselle Jennifer Walker: Thank you for believing in me with all your heart.

Contents

Part 1: Pertinent Bible Verses 1
Part 2: Metaphysics and New Thought 11
Part 3: Spiritual Procreation 28
Part 4: Universal Purpose 46
Part 5: The Still Light 91
Part 6: Etheric Materialization Into Form 100

Addendum: Author Presentations 132

Etheric Materialization Into Form!

Part 1: Pertinent Bible Verses

There are many Biblical passages that shed light onto this topic. We see the terms: Light, Faith, Truth, Love, etc. What do these terms mean? I have listed just four words. It may take a lifetime or more just to acquire an understanding of these four words. Now, I am not suggesting that one must be a "born-again Christian" to be able to manifest, i.e., bring your desire into material form. Nor am I suggesting one be a "born-again Christian," or be of any religious faith, for one to be "saved." But I am suggesting that there is a path forward for you and I to manifest that which is of our desire—and it is open to all.

Let's begin with this one thought. *Blessed are the pure in heart: for they shall see God.* This is **Matthew 5:8**. We can begin here with the understanding that to truly manifest one must have a *clean heart*. And what does a clean heart mean? Well, let us suggest that it means doing to another what you would have another do unto you. It means: love ye one another. It implies that that which we do affects others; and, in fact, will be done back to us. We have cause-effect action in play here. We have an interconnectivity in play.

Below is a list of Biblical verses that have encouraged me. You don't need to read them all at once. Find one you like and meditate on it. Or create your own list.

Genesis 1:3: And God said, Let there be light: and there was light.

Jeremiah 29:13: And ye shall seek me, and find me, when you shall search for me with all your heart.

Matthew 5:8: Blessed are the pure in heart: for they shall see God.

Matthew 5:16: Let your light so shine before men, that they may see your good works, and glorify your Father, which is in heaven.

Matthew 5:44: But I say unto you, Love your enemies, bless them that curse you, do good to them that hate you, and pray for them which despitefully use you, and persecute you.

Matthew 5:48: Be ye therefore perfect, even as your Father which is in heaven is perfect.

Matthew 21:22: And all things, whatsoever ye shall ask in prayer, believing, ye shall receive.

Matthew 22:37-40: Thou shalt love the Lord thy God with all thy heart, and with all thy soul, and with all thy mind. This is the first and great commandment. And the second is like unto it, thou shalt love thy neighbour as thyself. On these two commandments hang all the law and the prophets.

Matthew 24:35: Heaven and earth shall pass away, but my words shall not pass away.

Mark 5:30, 34: ...Who touched my clothes? ...Daughter, thy faith hath made thee whole; go in peace, and be whole of thy plague.

Mark 7:15: There is nothing from without a man, that entering into him can defile him: but the things which come out of him, those are they that defile the man.

Mark 10:27: With men *it is* impossible, but not with God: for with God all things are possible.

Mark 11:24: Therefore I say unto you, What things soever ye desire, when ye pray, believe that ye receive *them*, and ye shall have *them*.

Luke 6:27-28: Love your enemies, do good to them which hate you. Bless them that curse you, and pray for them which despitefully use you.

Luke 11: 9-10: And I say unto you, Ask, and it shall be given you; seek, and ye shall find; knock, and it shall be opened unto you. For every one that asketh receiveth; and he that seeketh findeth; and to him that knocketh it shall be opened.

Luke 17:20-21: The kingdom of God cometh not with observation: Neither shall they say, Lo here! Or lo there! For, behold, the kingdom of God is within you.

Luke 17:25: But first must he suffer many things, and be rejected of this generation.

Luke 18:27: The things which are impossible with men are possible with God.

Luke 23:34: Father, forgive them; for they know not what they do.

Luke 23:46: Father, unto thy hands I commend my spirit.

John 1:1-3: In the beginning was the Word, and the Word was with God, and the Word was God. The same was in the beginning with God. All things were made by him; and without him was not anything made that was made.

John 1:4: In him was life; and the life was the light of men.

John 1:5: And the light shineth in darkness; and the darkness comprehended it not.

John 1:9: That was the true light, which lighteth every man that cometh into the world.

John 3:3: Verily, verily, I say unto thee, Except a man be born again, he cannot see the kingdom of God.

John 4:24: God is a Spirit: and they that worship him must worship him in spirit and in truth.

John 6:38: For I came down from heaven, not to do mine own will, but the will of him that sent me.

John 6:47: Verily, verily, I say unto you, He that believeth on me hath everlasting life.

John 8:12: I am the light of the world: he that followeth me shall not walk in darkness, but shall have the light of life.

John 8:32: And ye shall know the truth, and the truth shall make you free.

John 8:45: And because I tell you the truth, ye believe me not.

John 9:5: As long as I am in the world, I am the light of the world.

John 10:30: I and my Father are one.

John 14:1: Let not your heart be troubled: ye believe in God, believe also in me.

John 14: 6: I am the way, the truth, and the life: no man cometh unto the Father, but by me.

John 14: 12: Verily, verily, I say unto you, He that believeth on me, the works that I do shall he do also; and greater works than these shall he do; because I go unto my Father.

John 14: 27: Peace I leave with you, my peace I give unto you: not as the world giveth, give I unto you. Let not your heart be troubled, neither let it be afraid.

John 15: 12: This is my commandment, That ye love one another, as I have loved you.

John 15: 13: Greater love hath no man than this, that a man lay down his life for his friends.

John 16: 12: I have yet many things to say unto you, but ye cannot bear them now.

Acts 20:35: It is more blessed to give than to receive.

I Corinthians 13:4-7,13: Love bears all things, believes all things, hopes all things, endures all things. Love never ends...So faith, hope, love abide, these three; but the greatest of these is love.

I Corinthians 15:17: And if Christ be not raised, your faith is vain; ye are yet in your sins.

II Corinthians 5:7: For we walk by faith, not by sight.

Ephesians 5:13: All things, when they are admitted, are made manifest by the light: for everything that is made manifest is light.

Philippians 1:2: Grace be unto you, and peace, from God our Father, and from the Lord Jesus Christ.

Philippians 1:3-4: I thank God whenever I think of you; and when I pray for you, my prayers are always joyful.

Philippians 4: 6-7: Be careful for nothing; but in everything by prayer and supplication with thanksgiving let your requests be made known unto God. And the peace of God, which passeth all understanding, shall keep your hearts and minds through Christ Jesus.

Philippians 4: 13: I can do all things through Christ which strengthens me.

Hebrews 11: 1: Now faith is the substance of things hoped for, the evidence of things not seen.

1 John 1: 5: God is light; in him there is no darkness.

1 John 4: 7: Beloved, let us love one another: for love is of God; and every one that loveth is born of God, and knowweth God.

1 John 4: 8: He that loveth not knoweth not God; for God is love.

1 John 4: 12: No man hath seen God at any time. If we love one another, God dwelleth in us, and his love is perfected in us.

1 John 4:16: And we have known and believed the love that God hath to us. God is love; and he that dwelleth in love dwelleth in God, and God in him.

1 John 4:18: There is no fear in love: but perfect love casteth out fear: because fear hath torment. He that feareth is not made perfect in love.

1 John 4:20: If a man say, I love God, and hateth his brother, he is a liar: for he that loveth not his brother whom he hath seen, how can he love God whom he that not seen?

1 John 4:21: And this commandment have we from him, That he who loveth God love his brother also.

I present these verses as an opening for the clarity of what is required of you, or anyone, to bring materialization to their hopes and desires. These verses shed light on and support the verse: *Blessed are the pure in heart: for they shall see God* from **Matthew 5:8**. Purity of heart is an internal necessity. The verse **1 John 4:18** states: *There is no fear in love: but perfect love casteth out fear: because fear hath torment. He that feareth is not made perfect in love.* Here we see another term for *pure in heart*. It is called *perfect love*.

Here is another verse, **1 John 1: 5:** *God is light; in him there is no darkness.* Might not *light,* which it is suggested in this verse comprises the very nature of God, be similar to *pure in heart* and *perfect love*? I believe so. **1 John 4:16** states that *God is love*. I guess then that *light* is also *love*. And look at all the things love is as presented in **I Corinthians 13:4-7,13:** *Love bears all things, believes all things, hopes all things, endures all things. Love never ends...So faith, hope, love abide, these three; but the greatest of these is love.* Do you see the connections? **Hebrews 11: 1** states: *How* *faith is the substance of things hoped for, the evidence of things not seen.* Now imagine the faith it takes to manifest your desires into form!

Let's take another example, this time from **Philippians 4: 13:** *I can do all things through Christ which strengthens me.* Could we equally say, *I can do all things through Light which strengthens me*—or *through Love which strengthens me*—or *through Faith which strengthens me*? Might I suggest that the term Christ is not to be associated to only one person, as in Jesus Christ, but is open for all to receive. If you are *pure in heart* you, too, are a Christ. If you have *perfect love* you are a Christ. If you have a *faith* that is stronger than a lack of evidence you are a Christ. If you can forgive another you are a Christ. Do you see the point? We make a mistake in suggesting, even demanding, that Jesus is the only Christ.

And one final example. Look at the four verses below.

Matthew 5:16: Let your light so shine before men, that they may see your good works, and glorify your Father, which is in heaven.

Matthew 5:44: But I say unto you, Love your enemies, bless them that curse you, do good to them that hate you, and pray for them which despitefully use you, and persecute you.

Matthew 5:48: Be ye therefore perfect, even as your Father which is in heaven is perfect.

John 14: 12: Verily, verily, I say unto you, He that believeth on me, the works that I do shall he do also; and greater works than these shall he do; because I go unto my Father.

I have heard so many times how there is only one Christ and that is Jesus. But did not Jesus himself utter the words *"Be ye therefore perfect, even as your Father which is in heaven is perfect"*? Would he say that if it was not possible? *Perfection*, like the terms *Light, Faith, Truth,* and *Love,* exists within us all. It is just a matter of getting to that mind, or heart, space inside ourselves. Why is this point important? Because in elevating Jesus, or anyone, above yourself or another you create an imbalance in the spiritual/energy field. To suggest that anyone is somehow metaphysically above you or beneath you, imbalances your etheric field. Look around, how many of us worship some type of "deity," also called a "divinity"? For the most part, our whole religious structure is based on a ranking: a creator God or Supreme Being which we are called to worship/bow down to. And yet Jesus also stated "...*He that beleiveth on me, the works that I do shall he do also; and greater works than these shall he do....*" Why would he say this if he considered you or me to be of lessor importance in life? Do you really think you are saved if you place some perceived "deity" before another; some "Chosen One"? How about the Prophet, Pope, or Imam? Somehow, they are to be considered as "holier than thou" intermediaries between ourselves and "God." We see the same in the political arena—the King or Queen, or President, etc., is viewed as more important than you or I. Whom is serving who here?

I, myself, was raised in a Christian home. In my youth, it seemed as if the most important verse in the Bible was **John 3:16:** *For God so loved the world, that he gave his only begotten Son, that whosoever believeth in him should not perish, but have everlasting life.* I often wondered, is there or can there be only one begotten Son? There is also the verse, **I Corinthians 15:17:** *And if Christ be not raised, your faith is vain; ye are yet in your sins.* As I grew up, I could not help but notice how this minister or that preacher was viewed as just a little more in the know as to how we must believe in the one and only "Christ Jesus" if we are to be saved. But won't my love for my parents count? How about my parent's love for me? Is that a secondary love? So we are to place Christ Jesus in the first position and, in this case, my love for my parents in the second position. I remember one time later in life I was speaking with my Dad. He was speaking about Jesus. Suddenly, I exclaimed, *"Dad, I love you as much as I love Jesus."* Well, he had the courtesy not to say, "You bad." In fact, he embraced my love as I did his. To him, I was a primary as he was to me. What stood out was that we had a moment where we simply shared our love for each other. And I ask, is not that <u>perfect love</u>? *Be ye therefore perfect, even as your Father which is in heaven is perfect.* I would suggest it is. Please don't equate your love for another as some secondary love. It is pure and holy love. I mean, think about it, how can a Father's love for his child be some secondary love. Or a Mother's love. Pure and unconditional! **1 John 4:12:** *"No man hath seen God at any time. If we love one another, God dwelleth in us, and his love is perfected in us."*

Just a last thought; I stated that I was raised in a Christian home. That Christianity was under the umbrella of Protestantism. This was in contrast to Catholicism. I don't know that there is a great difference between the two. St. Augustine (340-430), certainly influential in the development of the Catholic Church, believed in salvation through faith, not acts. Then there is Martin Luther (1483-1546), German theologian, known for the Protestant Reformation and Ninety-five Thesis, who was excommunicated from the Catholic Church. But he, too, believed in salvation through faith (divine grace) and not deeds. As I understand it, the fissure stemmed around the use of indulgences. Martin Luther "...condemned the excesses and corruption of the Roman Catholic Church, especially the papal practice of asking for payment—called 'indulgences'—for the forgiveness of sins."* So we have two issues here, faith as to works and indulgences. For a long time, I did not believe in faith, at least not a blind faith, a faith that could be in anything, i.e., supernatural, where 2 + 2 could = 5, or even that Jesus was the only Son of God. But then are we left with science which itself hardly has a beginning point. Somehow their "proofs" don't touch the heart of things; don't touch the soul.

*Taken from the internet, Wikipedia.

Henry David Thoreau (1817-1862)
"With all your science, can you tell me how it is that light comes into the soul?"

And I certainly was not in favor of indulgences as if we have to pay our way into "Heaven." But what I did get from St. Augustine and Martin Luther was that we, you and I, could have a <u>direct connection/communication</u> with God. We don't need an intermediary, not the Pope nor Prophet; not the Imam, guru nor sage, not the master nor mystic, not a King nor a Queen, and certainly not a politician. And this includes even Jesus. Listen to this quote from the artist, scientist, and philosopher Walter Russell.*

*I spent many years with the Walter and Lao Russell writings. I was also able to meet Lao Russell two times at the University of Science and Philosophy.

Walter Russell (1871-1963)—*The Universal One*, 1926

"Man conceives a perfect and omnipotent God. A perfect and omnipotent God could not create imperfection. He could not create lesser than Himself. He could not create greater than Himself. God could not create other than Himself, nor greater, nor lesser than Himself."

And then there is this beautiful quote from Walt Whitman.

Walt Whitman (1819-1892) *Leaves of Grass: Song for Myself* 1855

"I swear I see now that everything has an eternal soul! The trees have, rooted in the ground....the weeds of the sea have....the animals.

"I swear I think there is nothing but immortality! That the exquisite scheme is for it, and the nebulous float is for it, and the cohering is for it, And all preparation is for it...the identity is for it, and life and death are for it."

He also states:

"I celebrate myself, and sing myself, And what I assume you shall assume, For every atom belonging to me as good belongs to you."

This led me to metaphysics— "...the branch of philosophy that deals with the first principles of things, including abstract concepts such as being, knowing, substance, cause, identity, time, and space....they would regard the question of the initial conditions for the universe as belonging to the realm of metaphysics or religion."* It also led me to the New Thought movement.

*Definition from Oxford Languages.

Part 2: Metaphysics and New Thought

Metaphysics is about the pursuit of truth. By truth I mean the capital T Truth. It seeks the primary, the beginning, the universal, and the self-evident. I refer to this as the <u>Given</u>. We might just call it the *self-evident Given*. For example, existence exists.* Can we deny that? Hardly. Or, from a conscious point of view, "I Am." Right here we can surmise that existence and consciousness are necessary realities for there to be life. Moreover, we don't or can't prove this. It is self-evident, our beginning point from which we step forward. I mentioned earlier that science has yet to prove the existence of the Ether. Science can't prove the Ether for the Ether is but the Unity of all things. There isn't any differentiation in Unity. You can't prove absolute Unity but we must begin from there or, if not, from somewhere else. We run into the same issue with the term Spirit or Soul. Can we prove the existence of these things?** And yet something is occurring in life called **Life**.

*Taken from Objectivist philosophy of Ayn Rand.

**Remember the Henry David Thoreau quote from the last section.

Let's look at this quote from St. Augustine.

St. Augustine (354 - 430)
"Miracles are not contrary to nature, but only contrary to what we know about nature."

Just think about the term <u>nature</u>. It is being used here subsuming a fundamental nature/order to things. Again, aren't these assumptions necessary? How can any of us think, or even BE, without the necessity of a self-evident Given? Our fundamental existence subsumes Order; it subsumes Existence; it subsumes Consciousness! I would further suggest that it subsumes Life itself! So let us keep in mind that there is a fundamental <u>Order to Life</u>. We will be coming back to this topic.

New Thought* holds that *"Infinite Intelligence, or God, is everywhere, spirit is the totality of real things, true human selfhood is divine, divine thought is a source for good, sickness originates in the mind, and "right thinking" has a healing effect."***

*Also known as Cosmic Consciousness.
**Taken from the internet, Wikipedia.

Some further ideas or characteristics from New Thought are:

-There is only one mind/substance.

-God is life (or life force).

-Life is a creative process.

-All is perfection.

-The Law (of Attraction) is absolute.

-P.P. Quinby* **(1802-1866)** was an American folk healer, mentalist, and mesmerist. His work is widely recognized as foundational to the New Thought spiritual movement.

*Taken from the internet, Wikipedia.

The main tenet I take away from New Thought is that we, too, are a part of the God process. In Christian terms, we would say that each one of us is an only begotten Son or only begotten Daughter. Not just Jesus but you and I as well. **John 15: 12:** *"This is my commandment, That ye love one another, as I have loved you."* The same holds true for the idea of a "chosen people." There isn't a chosen people. Everyone is a chosen person. There isn't a chosen religion either. Religions are only metaphysical attempts at Truth. They rise or fall as to their alignment to Truth. Let's follow this up with another quote from Walter Russell and another Biblical verse.

Walter Russell (1871-1963)—*The Universal One*, 1926
"Light as man knows light, is but an unstable simulation of the real light of the Universal One. Man's concept of light is luminosity, an illusion of the universal light of inertia, sustained in its appearance as an illusion of light by the pressures generated through motion. The inner mind of ecstatic man knows the real light and that he is One with light. He is not deceived by its illusion."

1 John 1:5: God is light; in him there is no darkness.

So, if God is light and the inner mind of ecstatic man knows the real light and that he is One with light, then are not we all of the divine essence? Notice how there are two levels to the idea of Light. There is what we commonly know as physical light. Then there is the **Spiritual Light**. It is in this Spiritual Light that we are able to "Love ye one another"? Your love as well as my love is divine love.

Let's look to some examples from some New Thought writers:

Florence Scovel Shinn (1871-1940)—*The Game of Life and How to Play It*, 1925

"Only that which is true of God is true of me, for I and the Father are ONE.

"As I am one with God, I am one with my good, for God is both the *Giver* and the *Gift*. I cannot separate the *Giver* from the *Gift*.

"Every plan my Father in heaven has not planned, shall be dissolved and dissipated, and the Divine Idea now comes to pass.

"Divine love now dissolves and dissipates every wrong condition in my mind, body, and affairs. Divine love is the most powerful chemical in the universe, and *dissolves everything* which is not of itself!"

Florence Scovel Shinn (1871-1940)—*Forgiveness Affirmation Meditation*

"I call on the law of forgiveness. I am free from mistakes and the consequences of mistakes. I am under grace and not under karmic law. I forgive everyone and everyone forgives me. The gates swing open for my good."

Elizabeth Bellhouse—*Measureless Healing*

"If we are to live in God and God in us, then we must become as aware as we can be of the nature of that in which we live and move and have our being. That which indwells us, permeates all our being, and surrounds us before and behind, to the right, and to the left, and is above us, and beneath us. That which is *both the First Principle and the Upholding Principle of the whole scheme of Creation."*

" *'Make your home in Me',* he said continuing the same theme, *'as I make mine in you. If you remain in me and my words remain in you, you may ask what you will and you shall get it. Believe the works for they prove the Father is in me and that I am in Him. The Father has given Me power over all flesh.'"*

Joseph Benner (1872-1938)—*The Impersonal Life*, 1914

"But both you who comprehend and you who fear, know that I AM even now manifesting My Will thru you; and the time will surely come when you will know no other Will but mine, and when all things *You* Will, will come to pass and you will awaken fully from your Dream of Separation, and know Me as your Real and only Self.

"But this will not be until you have given yourself and everything in your life wholly over to Me, and there is nothing left in *your* human personality to attract from others the slightest inharmonious thought or feeling, by act or word of yours.

"Your way *then* will be one continuous round of blessing. Wherever you go will My Light shine and My Love radiate forth about you, creating Peace, Concord, Unity. And the great thing will be, tho not great but natural when once you understand, that everyone will be better and happier by reason of your appearance in their lives."

Meister Eckhart (1260-1327)

"In the eternal birth, the soul becomes pure and one."

"All creatures are interdependent."

"Relation is the essence of everything that is."

"Everything is full and pure at its source and precisely there, not outside."

"When God lights the soul with wisdom, it floods the faculties, and the man knows more than ever could be taught him."

"The outward work will never be puny if the inward work is great."

Meister Eckhart (1260-1327)—*Selections from His Essential Writings*

"...The Father gives birth to his Son without ceasing; and I say more: he gives me birth—me, his Son and the same son. I say more: He gives birth not only to me, his Son, but he gives birth to me as himself and himself as me and to me as his being and nature. In the innermost source, there I spring out in the Holy Spirit, where there is one life and one being and one work. Everything God performs is one; therefore he gives me, his Son, birth without any distinction."

"...The Father gives his Son birth without ceasing. Once the Son has been born he receives nothing from the Father because he has it all, but what he receives from the Father is his being born."

"...Then the angel said: "The Holy Spirit will come down from above into you, from the highest throne, from the Father of eternal light."

"All created things act according to their first purity and according to their highest perfection."

Neville Goddard (1905-1972)—*Resurrection*, 1966

"If you knew how you would feel were you to realize your objective, then, inversely, you would know what state—you could realize were you to awaken in yourself such a feeling. The injunction, to pray believing that you already possess what you pray for, is based upon a knowledge of the Law of Inverse Transformation. If your realized prayer produces in you a definite feeling or state of consciousness, then, inversely, that particular feeling or state of consciousness must produce your realized prayer. Because all transformations of force are reversible, you should always assume the feeling of your fulfilled wish.

You should awaken within you the feeling that you are and have that which heretofore you desired to be and possess. This is easily done by contemplating the joy that would be yours were your objective an accomplished fact, so that you live and move and have your being in the feeling that your wish is realized.

"Assume the feeling of your wish fulfilled and continue feeling that it is fulfilled unto that which you feel objectifies itself. If a physical fact can produce a psychological state, a psychological state can produce a physical fact. If the effect (a) can be produced by the cause (b), then inversely, the effect (b) can be produced by the cause (a). 'Therefore I say unto you, What things soever ye desire when ye pray, believe that ye have received them, and ye shall have them.' (Mark 11: 24)

"When you emerge from prayer you no longer seek, for you have—if you have prayed correctly—subconsciously assumed the reality of the state sought, and by the Law of Reversibility your subconscious assumption must objectify that which it affirms."

Genevieve Behrend (1881-1960)—*Your Invisible Power: The Mental Science of Thomas Troward*, 1951

"The best there is, is mine. There is no limit to me, because my mind is a center of divine operation, and your picture is as certain to come true, in your physical world, as the sun is to shine."

"This same power that brought universal substance into existence will bring your individual thought or mental picture into physical form."

"The Originating Principle is not in any way dependent upon any person, place, or thing. It has no past and knows no future. The law is that the Originating Creative Principle of Life is the universal here and now."

"The Idea must contain within itself the only one and primary substance there is, and this means money as well as everything else."

"My mind is a center of Divine operation. The Divine operation is always for expansion and fuller expression, and this means the production of something beyond what has gone before, something entirely new, not included in the past experience, though proceeding out of it by an orderly sequence of growth. Therefore, since the Divine cannot change its inherent nature, it must operate in the same manner with me; consequently, in my own special world, of which I am the center, it will move forward to produce new conditions, always in advance of any that have gone before."

"That is to say, you light up your desire with absolute faith that the Creative Spirit of Life, in you, is doing the work. By the steady flow of the light of the Will on the Spirit, your desired picture is projected upon the screen of the physical world—an exact reproduction of the pictured slide in your mind."

"This same power that brought universal substance into existence will bring your individual thought or mental picture into physical form. There is no difference in the power. The only difference is a difference of degree. The power and the substance themselves are the same. Only in working out your mental picture, it has transferred its creative energy from the Universal to the particular, and is working in the same unfailing manner from its specific center, your mind."

John McDonald (1906-1998)—*The Message of the Master,* 1929

"There are no limits to my possibilities! My successes will multiply and increase in proportion to my mastery of the Law."

"I operate according to a definite, unerring law. I know the outcome before I start."

"Any picture firmly held in any mind, in any form, is bound to come forth. That is the great, unchanging Universal Law that, when we cooperate with it intelligently, makes us absolute masters of the conditions and situations in our lives."

"It is a false belief that there is a power or powers outside you greater than the power within you."

"The consciousness or fixed picture in mind of anything, any condition, any circumstance is the actual thing itself."

"We have the capacity and the power to create desirable pictures within, and to find them automatically printed in the outer world of our surroundings."

"When you invoke the aid of this law, you do not need money, friends, or influence to attain whatever your heart is set upon. It doesn't matter in the least what your position is in life. It doesn't matter whether your ambition is directly in line with the position you now occupy, or whether it requires a complete change from what you are doing. You may have no definite plan in life except the fact that you want to get ahead. All the desire in the world will get you nowhere; what is necessary to do first is to establish a *set definite objective* firmly within."

Glenn Clark (1882-1956)—*The Thought Farthest Out*

"Prayer, in so far as you hope it will change the outward conditions about you, must first of all change conditions within you."

"It doesn't matter to whom or to what one gives oneself—it only matters HOW one gives oneself. The light—the love—the joy—the abundance with which you give yourself attracts the same that is outside of you to you. It cannot be otherwise."

"What shall you give? Most beautiful, most powerful, most wonderful of all gifts is yourself, your faith, your trust, your love. Trust men, trust God, trust events. And the most powerful, most beautiful of all giving is forgiving your enemies, your persecutors. If you really do that once, then you become irresistible. After that you will draw all things to you. For then you are perfect even as your heavenly Father is perfect."

"For again let me repeat: You attract unto yourself the condition that accords with what you are; and if you are perfect, you draw perfection to you."

"Do not have Love. Be Love. And then you will attract all the Goodness, all the Perfection that the world has in store for you to you; You will draw the very Kingdom of Heaven itself down to the earth. When your Power to love becomes like God's power to Love, then your Power to create will become like God's Power to create."

"...And the moment that you become love, thenceforth whatever you ask shall be yours. Whatever you expect shall be yours. Whatever you want shall be yours. For you shall thenceforth ask for, and expect, and want, only that which is in accord with the spirit of infinite love. For you are love and love is the power that draws all things into perfectly adjusted and harmonious activity. You henceforth attract unto you the condition that accords with what you are."

"Thenceforth you are love and all the principalities and powers cannot then separate you from the Love of God. ...And the moment that you become love, thenceforth whatever you ask shall be yours. Whatever you expect shall be yours. Whatever you want shall be yours. For you shall thenceforth ask for, and expect, and want, only that which is in accord with the spirit of infinite love. For you are love and love is the power that draws all things into perfectly adjusted and harmonious activity. You henceforth attract unto you the condition that accords with what you are."

Robert Collier (1885-1950)

"All power is from within and therefore under our control."

"See things that you want as already yours. Know that they will come to you at need. Then let them come. Don't fret and worry about them. Don't think about your lack of them. Think of them as yours, as belonging to you, as already in your possession."

"The essence of this law is that you must think abundance; see abundance, feel abundance, believe abundance. Let no thought of limitation enter your mind."

"If you have any lack, if you are prey to poverty or disease, it is because you do not believe or do not understand the power that is yours. It is not a question of the Universal giving to you. It offers everything to everyone—there is no partiality."

Ralph Waldo Emerson (1803-1882)

"Thought is the blossom; language is the bud; action the fruit behind it."

"Great men are they who see that spiritual is stronger than material force, that thoughts rule the world."

Charles Fillmore (1854-1948)

"The spiritual substance from which comes all visible wealth is never depleted. It is right with you all the time and responds to your faith in it and your demands on it."

"Divine Mind is the one and only reality."

Charles Haanel (1866-1949)

"There is no limit to what this law can do for you; dare to believe in your own ideal; think of the ideal as an already accomplished fact."

"The real secret of power is consciousness of power."

"The absolute truth is that the 'I' is perfect and complete; the real 'I' is spiritual and can therefore never be less than perfect; it can never have any lack, limitation, or disease."

"The vibrations of mental forces are the finest and consequently the most powerful in existence."

"The predominant thought or the mental attitude is the magnet, and the law is that like attracts like, consequently, the mental attitude will invariably attract such conditions as correspond to its nature."

"It is the combination of thought and love which forms the irresistible force of the law of attraction."

"Remember, and this is one of the most difficult as well as most wonderful statements to grasp. Remember that no matter what the difficulty is, no matter where it is, no matter who is affected, you have no patient but yourself; you have nothing to do but convince yourself of the truth which you desire to see manifested."

"The principle which gives the thought the dynamic power to correlate with its object, and therefore to master every adverse human experience, is the law of attraction, which is another name for love. This is an eternal and fundamental principle inherent in all things, in every system of philosophy, in every Religion and in every Science. There is no getting away from the law of love. It is feeling that imparts vitality to thought. Feeling is desire and desire is love. Thought impregnated with love becomes invincible."

"The universal Mind is not only intelligence, but it is substance, and this substance is the attractive force which brings electrons together by the law of attraction so they form atoms; the atoms in turn are brought together by the same law and form molecules; molecules take objective forms and so we find that the law is the creative force behind every manifestation, not only of atoms, but of worlds, of the Universe, of everything of which the imagination can form any conception."

"To become conscious of this power is to become a 'live wire.' The Universe is the live wire. It carries power sufficient to meet every situation in the life of every individual. When the individual mind touches the Universal Mind, it receives all its power."

Henry Thomas Hamblin (1873-1958)

"Sooner or later, just when we are ready for it, opportunity comes our way, just as surely as the rising and setting of the sun. The law is infallible. When we are ready the opportunity appears."

Earnest Holmes (1887-1960)—*The Science of Mind*

"In treating we conceive of the ultimate of the idea but never of the process. Never treat a process. We plant a seed and there is in the seed, operating through the creative soil, everything that will cause it to develop, unfold and produce a plant. *The ultimate of effect is already potential in its cause.* This is the mystical meaning of the words: 'I am Alpha and Omega.' Our word for the fullest expression of our life or for its smallest detail should be the alpha and omega, the beginning and the end of the thing thought of. All cause and effect are in Spirit, they are bound together in one complete whole. One is the inside, the other the outside of the same thing."

"Never let anything cause you to doubt your ability to demonstrate the Truth. CONCEIVE OF YOUR WORD AS BEING THE THING. See the desire as an already accomplished fact and rest in perfect confidence, peace and certainty, never looking for results, never wondering, never becoming anxious, never being hurried nor worried. Those who do not understand this attitude may think you are inactive but remember: 'To him who can perfectly practice inaction, all things are possible.'"

"What we know about Subjective Mind proves that It is unconscious of time, knows neither time nor process. *It knows only the completion, the answer.* That is why it is written, 'Before they call, I will answer.' Cosmic Creation is from idea not object. It does not know anything about process; process is involved in it but not consciously. Correct practice should know that ultimate right action is now, today. If we say, 'Tomorrow it is going to be,' then according to the very law we are using we hold the answer in the state of futurity which can never become present. If a gardener holds his seed in his hand and says, 'Tomorrow I am going to plant this seed,' his garden will never start growing. Therefore, Jesus said: 'When ye pray, believe that ye have and ye shall receive.' He did not say believe and you will immediately have. He said, 'Ye shall receive.' He did not deny the natural law of evolution and growth. Nature operates according to a law of logical sequence."

"Bring out the idea of Substance. Make consciousness perceive that Substance is Spirit, Spirit is God, and God is all there is. Once you acquaint the consciousness with this idea, it is implanted in the Creative power, which is externalized in your life."

"Continue to declare there were no mistakes, there are none and there never will be. Say, 'I represent the Truth, the whole Truth and Nothing but the Truth.' It is unerring. It never makes mistakes. There are no mistakes in the Divine Plan for me. There is no limitation, poverty, want nor lack. I stand in the midst of eternal opportunity, which is forever presenting me with the evidence of its full expression. 'I am joy, peace and happiness. I am the spirit of joy within me. I am the spirit of happiness within me. I radiate Life: I am Life. There is One Life and that Life is my Life now.'"

"I expect, fully and emphatically, the answer to my prayer today. Right now do I possess this thing I so greatly desire. I remove my fear of lack and negation, for it is the only barrier which stands in the way of my experience of good. I alone can remove it. And I do remove it now."

"Today, in this moment, the Law responds to my thought. My word is one of affirmation, rising from the knowledge that the Good, the Enduring and the True are Eternalities in my experience. I cannot be apart from that which is my good. My good is assured me by God, the Indwelling Essence of my life."

"All the good that you desire awaits your acceptance of it."

Vernon Howard (1918-1992)
"What you want also wants you. There are no unanswered requests in the universe. If we do not like what we are receiving, we can learn to ask for something different. Then we will find what we wish."

"Resistance to the disturbance is the disturbance."

William James (1842-1910)
"The greatest discovery of my generation is that human beings can alter their lives by altering their attitudes of mind."

Christian D. Larson (1874-1954)

"That a man can change himself...and master his own destiny is the conclusion of every great mind who is wide-awake to the power of right thought."

"To begin to move forward is to begin to make real the ideal, and we will realize in the now as much of the ideal as is necessary to make the now full and complete. To move forward steadily during the great eternal now is to eternally become more than you are; and to become more than you are is to make yourself more and more like your ideal; and here is the great secret, because the principle is that you will realize your ideal when you become exactly like your ideal, and that you will realize as much of your ideal now as you develop in yourself now."

Prentice Mulford (1834-1891)

"Every thought of yours is a real thing—a force."

Walter Russell (1871-1963)

"Idea cannot evade its manifestation into form."

"All questions are answerable in the light; thou art light."

Wallace Wattles (1860-1911)—*The Science of Getting Rich*, 1910

"There is a thinking stuff from which all things are made, and which, in its original state, permeates, penetrates, and fills the interspaces of the universe.

"A thought in this substance produces the thing that is imaged by the thought.

"Man can form things in his thought, and, by impressing his thought upon formless substance, can cause the thing he thinks about to be created.

"In order to do this, man must pass from the competitive to the creative mind; he must form a clear mental picture of the things he wants, and must do with faith of purpose, all that can be done each day, doing each separate thing in an efficient matter."

"Many people who order their lives rightly in all other ways are kept in poverty by their lack of gratitude."

Walt Whitman (1819-1892)

"I do not doubt that whatever can possibly happen anywhere at any time, is provided for in the inherences of things."

"Why, who makes much of a miracle? As to me I know nothing else but miracles—To me every hour of night and day is a miracle, Every cubic inch of space a miracle."

Peter V. Ross—*If A Man Die He Shall Live Again*, 1945

"It was never made or created; it always was, it always will be. Its origin cannot be determined, its extinction cannot be conceived, its confines cannot be crossed. For this is a living not a lifeless world. Life not only pervades the universe; it is the universe."

"The spiritual power thereby released reaches those who have crossed the bar. Prayer does not lose its efficacy or fail its destination because one party is asleep and the other awake. It is not frustrated by walls, intervening distances, or varying states of consciousness. Not a single right thought ever goes forth in vain."

"What a comfort, following seasons of grief and speculation, for one to come back to the fundamental proposition that Life, the Life of man, is the forever I am, and to learn that individual existence is more than a link in the chain of Life, it is the chain itself."

P.P. Quimby (1802-1866) *The Quimby Manuscripts*, 1921

"A belief in a disease is like a belief in any other evil, but there are those who putting entire confidence in the leaders accept certain beliefs. Such are honest and are the hardest patients to cure, for they attach a religious respect to their beliefs which are their very life. They often say they would rather die than lose their belief."

"This was what Jesus tried to prove, so all His acts and talk went to prove the truth of what I have said. Make man responsible for his beliefs and he will be as cautious in what he believes as he is in what he sees or does, for he will see that just as he measures out to another so it will be measured out to him."

"Wisdom has no laws; it is the true light. The law of man is the invention of evil thoughts. In proportion as Wisdom is in us the law is dead. So to be wise is to be dead to the law. For law is man's belief and Wisdom is of God or Science. Now if we could understand the true idea of causes and effects, we could learn where the true cause of disease originated."

"All men have sinned or embraced beliefs, so all must die to their belief. Disease is a belief; health is in Wisdom. So as man dies to his belief he lives in Wisdom. My theory is to destroy death or belief and bring life and Wisdom into the world, therefore I come to the sick, not to save their beliefs or life in disease, but to destroy it. And he that loseth his belief for Wisdom will find his health or life."

"Religion was what crucified Christ. Pilate's wisdom found no fault with Him, but the religion of the priests said 'crucify him.'"

"Now where is the God in whose wisdom I believe? He is in the hearts of the people. He is not a man, neither has He form; He is neither male nor female."

"This power is called Christ or God and *if you have not this power or Christ you are not of Him.* To know God is to know ourselves, and to know ourselves is to have the difference between Science and error. Error is of man and truth is of God, and as truth is not in the cause of disease it is not in the effect."

"All the people believed in death. Jesus did not; therefore His arguments were to prove that death was a false idea. So if we believe in death we are in our belief, if we know it as an error we are in life. Jesus had to prove that what we call death was only separation of His Truth from the people's belief."

"Eternal life was taught to man by Jesus and called Christ instead of Science, and to know this Christ is to know eternal progress."

"Women have more endurance and more patience to investigate new science than man. And their wisdom is not of this world, but of that higher power called Science. When they give their idea to man, he then eats or understands, and then goes to work to form the idea that has been given to him by the woman. It has always been the case that all spiritual wisdom has been received through the female."

"When God said 'Let us create man in our own image,' it means Wisdom created man in the image of Truth. When He formed man or matter, that was the medium for this image to have and control, like all other living things that He made out of matter."

What may we surmise from all this?* May I suggest that at the core of New Thought is that we are created in his (God's) image: As P.P. Quimby noted: *"Let us create man in our own image."* But then there is the quote from Prentice Mulford: *"Every thought of yours is a real thing—a force."* I wonder, is God a force? A Creator God? A Living Force God? An Originating Creative Life Principle? Let us ask it this way, did **God** create life or is **Life** God? Furthermore, if our every thought a real thing, an actual *force*, must not there be a counterforce?

*For those interested the writing *Cosmic Consciousness: A Study in the Evolution of the Human Mind* by Richard Maurice Bucke, 1901, is a good read.

Part 3: Spiritual Procreation

Something is missing. What might that be? It is so close to us that we cannot see it. We create philosophies to understand; we create religions so we may believe; we create sciences so that we might prove. But we know not what. Again, listen to what P.P. Quimby stated:

> "All men have sinned or embraced beliefs, so all must die to their belief. Disease is a belief; health is in Wisdom. So as man dies to his belief he lives in Wisdom. My theory is to destroy death or belief and bring life and Wisdom into the world, therefore I come to the sick, not to save their beliefs or life in disease, but to destroy it. And he that loseth his belief for Wisdom will find his health or life."

> "Religion was what crucified Christ. Pilate's wisdom found no fault with Him, but the religion of the priests said 'crucify him.'"

> "Now where is the God in whose wisdom I believe? He is in the hearts of the people. He is not a man, neither has He form; He is neither male nor female."

> "Eternal life was taught to man by Jesus and called Christ instead of Science, and to know this Christ is to know eternal progress."

P.P. Quimby also stated:

> "Women have more endurance and more patience to investigate new science than man. And their wisdom is not of this world, but of that higher power called Science*. When they give their idea to man, he then eats or understands, and then goes to work to form the idea that has been given to him by the woman. It has always been the case that all spiritual wisdom has been received through the female."

*Quimby used the term Science more like we would use the term Wisdom.

> "When God said 'Let us create man in our own image,' it means Wisdom created man in the image of Truth. When

He formed man or matter, that was the medium for this image to have and control, like all other living things that He made out of matter."

Let us par this down one more time. Here are two of the above Quimby quotes:

"Now where is the God in whose wisdom I believe? He is in the hearts of the people. He is not a man, neither has He form; He is neither male nor female."

"Women have more endurance and more patience to investigate new science than man. And their wisdom is not of this world, but of that higher power called Science. When they give their idea to man, he then eats or understands, and then goes to work to form the idea that has been given to him by the woman. It has always been the case that all spiritual wisdom has been received through the female."

What are we to make of this? *"He [God] is neither male or female."* And yet, at the same time, *"And their [female] wisdom is not of this world, but of that higher power called Science. ...It has always been the case that all spiritual wisdom has been received through the female."* Historically, we have understood the necessity of male and female on the physical level. It takes a man and a woman to make a baby. That is self-evident although today the LGBTQ movement would like to suggest that there are many more sexes and sexual configurations then we have thought. Even on the mental level, of thought, we have recognized a differentiation between the two sexes. Having said that, even to suggest that men and women have different minds/thoughts is not so popular today; the feminists' having tried to say that men and women are mentally equal while at the same time holding to a uniqueness to themselves. I would suggest this confusion is due to our misunderstanding the spiritual level of things. Going back to the Quimby quote, *"He [God] is neither male or female."* Then what, or who, is God? Perhaps he/she is both male and female, an androgynous God. This would make some sense if we viewed "God" as the UNITY of all things. Like the ETHER, for example. Perhaps "God" is LIGHT, i.e., the spiritual LIGHT behind the physical light. In any event, we have a problem. It appears we have a "God" of a certain nature, different than the nature of ourselves. How are we ever to know anything? Well, perhaps there is a missing link to our understanding.

I would like to ask, assuming there is a missing link, what do you the reader think this missing link is? Let us go back to the Bible and review some verses, keeping in mind Walter Russell's earlier quote.

Walter Russell (1871-1963)—*The Universal One*, 1926
"Man conceives a perfect and omnipotent God. A perfect and omnipotent God could not create imperfection. He could not create lesser than Himself. He could not create greater than Himself. God could not create other than Himself, nor greater, nor lesser than Himself."

Genesis 1:3: And God said, Let there be light: and there was light.

Genesis 1:27: So God created man in his own image, in the image of God created he him, male and female created he them.

Genesis 2:24: Therefore shall a man leave his father and his mother, and shall cleave unto his wife: and they shall be one flesh.

Genesis 6:19: And of every living thing of all flesh, two of every sort shalt thou bring into the ark, to keep them alive with thee; they shall be male and female.

Matthew 19:4-6: Have ye not read, that he which made them in the beginning made them male and female, And said, for this cause shall a man leave father and mother, and shall cleave to his wife: and they twain shall be one flesh? Wherefore they are no more twain, but one flesh. What therefore God hath joined together, let not man put asunder.

Any ideas? Remember, the field of metaphysics is about 1st causes and a one Order. It is about absolute/self-evident TRUTH. Is this within our grasp? So, we are created in the image of God, i.e.,

"He could not create lesser than Himself. He could not create greater than Himself. God could not create other than Himself, nor greater, nor lesser than Himself." Furthermore, *"God created man in his own image, in the image of God created he him, male and female created he them."* And then we come to Matthew 19:4-6. It states that we are made male and female ***from the beginning!*** Moreover, *"for this cause shall a man leave father and mother, and shall cleave to his wife: and they twain shall be one flesh?"* Are you beginning to see an <u>order</u> taking shape? And it has a process in play, what we may call ***force-counterforce***. And we recognize this **Sexual Process**, at least to some degree on the physical and mental realms. But on the spiritual realm it, the Sexual Process, seems to disappear. Why is that? Some religions touch upon this. The verses in Genesis and Matthew touch upon it. Certainly, in Eastern thought, the Tao, with its forces of Yin and Yang, point to it.

Now let's look to what the great Hindu saint Sri Ramakrishna (1836-1886) said.

Sri Ramakrishna (1836-1886)—*A Bridge to Eternity: Sri Ramakrishna and His Monastic Order*, 1986

"I have long thought of telling you one thing, but have never done so yet. I want to tell you today. It is about my spiritual condition. You say that whoever will practice Sádhaná will realize it. That is not so. There is some specialty about it.

"She, Mother has spoken to me. I have not merely seen Her—She has also talked with me. I was at the Vat-talã. She came out of the Ganga to me. Oh, how She laughed! She played with my fingers and cracked them in fun. And then She spoke—She talked with me!

"I cried for three days at a time.—And She revealed to me all the contents of the Vedas, Puránas and Tantras...

"She, Mother has spoken to me. I have not merely seen Her—She has also talked with me." Here we have **Mother** speaking to Sri Ramakrishna. Is that Mother but an equal part of a Father/Mother God? And I don't mean a one Father/Mother God but TWO, a **Father God** and a **Mother God**. There are two things going on here—from the beginning. We can't have a singular "God" create a two things/sexes. The sexes themselves must be implanted into

the act of creation from the very beginning. **Genesis 1:27:** *So God created man in his own image, in the image of God created he him, male and female created he them.* As Walter Russell explains, *"He could not create lesser than Himself. He could not create greater than Himself. God could not create other than Himself, nor greater, nor lesser than Himself."* Can you capture the feeling of a Creative Process as God, and that it is not different from the **Sexual Process of Life** itself? There are samples of this Creative Process all down through history. My point is that these samples, although not complete, touch upon a **Sexual Creative Process of Life**. What we call **Sex** is actually a <u>Sexual Creative Process</u>. If you are following me, you will realize that this Sexual Creative Process is from the beginning. **Genesis 1:27:** *So God created man in his own image, in the image of God created he him, male and female created he them.* This is further to suggest that what we refer to as "God" is not some non-sexual/androgynous singular force of creation. **There isn't a singular force of creation.** What would that mean? Let me suggest, God is but a name we give to a beginning point that actually comprises a **two forces, a sexual process**. Could "God" create something that is not of his/her nature? *"He could not create lesser than Himself. He could not create greater than Himself. God could not create other than Himself, nor greater, nor lesser than Himself."* But even more than that this creative process consists of <u>two primary forces</u>. To suggest there is a Creator God who can create through or as a singular force is without merit. *"For every action there is an equal and opposite reaction."* *

*Newton's Third Law of Motion

    To date we have postulated a non-sexual creator God. By sex I mean two forces, equal and opposite. Clearly man and woman would be an example of these two forces, **equal and opposite**. Do we see this in the Quimby quotes?

> "Now where is the God in whose wisdom I believe? He is in the hearts of the people. He is not a man, neither has He form; He is neither male nor female."

> "Women have more endurance and more patience to investigate new science than man. And their wisdom is not of this world, but of that higher power called Science. When they give their idea to man, he then eats or

understands, and then goes to work to form the idea that has been given to him by the woman. It has always been the case that all spiritual wisdom has been received through the female."

Quimby suggests that *"He (God) is not a man, neither has He form; He is neither male nor female."* If so, how can "God" create man and woman—in his image no less? One more time, *"God could not create other than Himself, nor greater, nor lesser than Himself."* Does this imply that God is creating man (man and woman) in his image/likeness? And that there are two primary forces, male and female, equal and opposite, in play? It appears so. And, furthermore, the second Quimby quote states, *"Women have more endurance...their wisdom is not of this world....When they give their idea to man, he then eats or understands, and then goes to work to form the idea that has been given to him by the woman."* And, as a finale, *"It has always been the case that all spiritual wisdom has been received through the female."*

Interesting. Not so different from Sri Ramakrishna: *"She, Mother has spoken to me. I have not merely seen Her—She has also talked with me. I was at the Vat-talā. She came out of the Ganga to me. Oh, how She laughed! She played with my fingers and cracked them in fun. And then She spoke—She talked with me!"*

I understand I am being repetitive. But this is the issue—is "God" and Man and Woman of the same metaphysical nature? This is to say is God but a <u>name</u> for the **Two Forces Creative Process of Life**? Or is "God" some singular Godhead who creates man and woman separate from his nature and ways? If that is the case then what is the purpose of creating man and woman at all? That hasn't turned out so well, especially in light of the discrimination (women thought to be of lesser status than men) of woman? And even in religious societies! And yet a few men over the ages have stood up and spoke of the spiritual wisdom of women. Perhaps what we call the **Holy Spirit** is actually the soul of woman. I hope you, the reader, can see the importance of what may be called **Man and Woman Balance**. Not Man and Woman Equality, and certainly not DEI (Diversity, Equity, and Inclusion). The definition of Man and Woman Balance is **Equal and Opposite**.

Webster's New World Dictionary
Balance: A state of equilibrium or equipoise, equality in amount...as between two things. **Equilibrium:** A state of balance or equality between opposing forces.

"A state of balance or equality between opposing forces." This state of balance may be called the Law of Polarity or just Polar Opposites. You can't have an individualization of form without there being at the same moment and individualization of an equal and opposite other form. This is what male and female mean. "God" could not create male and female forces unless his/her own nature was of this **Two Forces Creative Process of Life**! Any act of creation must come from a balance or equality between opposing forces. There cannot be singular LIFE. LIFE is but an interaction between two equal and opposite forces. This is what I call **Man and Woman Balance**. Man and Woman Balance is simply an actual equal and opposite, i.e., **sexual** interconnection that brings forth new life. We are speaking here of a creative process without beginning or an ending. LIFE is Eternal Life! Do you understand? We can't even conceive of a one/singular force. We cannot comprehend a "sexless God." But we can comprehend a *balance or equality between opposing forces*, i.e., **a man and a woman creating life together**, begetting new life.

Webster's New World Dictionary
Procreant: Producing young; fruitful. Of procreation.
Procreate: To produce young; beget offspring; reproduce.
To produce or bring into existence.

So the issue at hand is LIFE itself. Must not we adhere to a metaphysic/order that holds to LIFE? Find me one religion that is based in the actual frame of LIFE. We acknowledge Sexual Balance and Procreation on the physical level, and even somewhat on the mental level, but at the spiritual level no such thing. We have not, if you will, viewed "God" as a sexual being. It would also require "God" not to be a singular entity/force but a **Procreant Process of**

***Two Forces**, Male and Female*. I have stated it this way.

Let's return to Walter Russell. I believe he, along with his wife Lao Russell, has come the closest to this SEXUAL articulation. Again, why is this so important? Because, right now, we have a discrepancy/divide. Our lives and God's life do not sync up together. And so we have all these different religions/philosophies that we continue to push on each other. We can't get to a balance or harmony together. What we have is GREED, THEFT, and WAR. And unless or until we get to the heart of this two-force (equal and opposite) sexual distinction, greed, theft and war it will continue to be.

Just so you know, I came to the Russell's writings in 1970 through Robert Birk who I met in college. He had come across the book *The Man Who Tapped The Secrets Of The Universe* by Glenn Clark, © 1946. Both of us were delighted by Glenn Clark's book. It led us to *The University of Science and Philosophy*. Lo and behold, we came upon a gold mind, that of the Russell's writings which altered the very course of our lives. I speak to this more in my writing *Selected Writings, Volume 3— A New Trinity.* For now, let's look at some quotes and drawings from the writings of Walter and Lao Russell.

Walter Russell (1871-1963)—*The Universal One*, 1926
"Sex is of all things from the beginning. Sex begins when light begins. Sex is the desire for the appearance of being which constitutes the appearance of existence. Nothing can be without the desire to be. All things are which desire to be. Desire dominates all thinking. Desire dominates all matter. All desire is sex desire."

Walter and Lao Russell—*Atomic Suicide?*, 1957
"The Father-Mother of Creation divides His sexless unity into sex-divided pairs of father and mother bodies, for the purpose of uniting them to create other pairs of father and mother bodies in eternal sequences forever."

Lao Russell (1904-1988)—*Why You Cannot Die: The Continuity of Life, Reincarnation Explained*, 1972

"Know thou that thou shalt know space, but never emptiness for:

"Behold! I am Space and I fill all of it.

"I am its One, its undivided Father-Mother One of my universe.

"I divide My oneness, and behold! I am two—father and mother.

"These two extend from Me, one on My right hand and one on My left.

"Each equally balanced with the other in the Oneness of their matehood.

"And then, behold! My two become one in Me, the One Father-Mother, undivided—

"To again become two to Father-Mother my eternal universe."

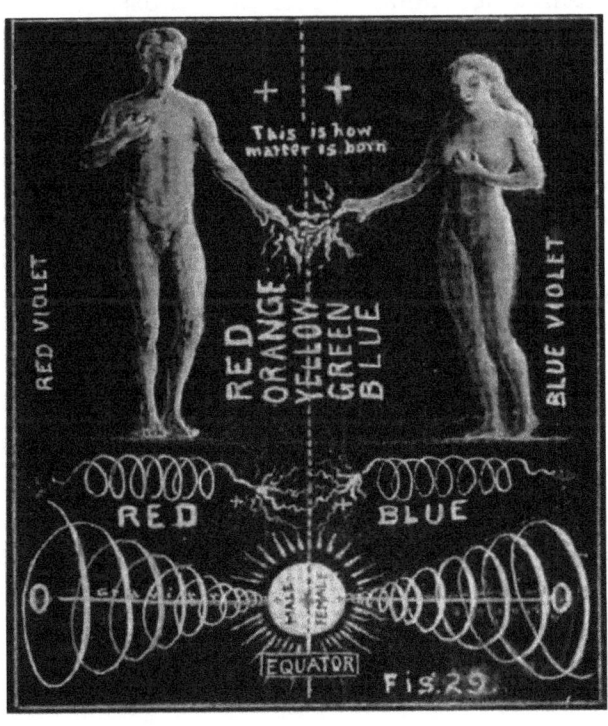

Walter and Lao Russell—*Home Study Course in Universal Law, Natural Science, and Living Philosophy, Unit 6, Lesson 22*, 1951

"Mankind has thought of sex in terms of a relation between the opposite sexes in organic living systems, never for a moment including sex relations in the mineral kingdom, in hot suns, or the ice caps of the poles of planets. We have used such terms as cohabitation and sex relation as though the sex relation is entirely separate and apart from other relations, and as though its reproductive effect is limited to living things that die or decay.

"From now on, sex will be regarded in our new perspective as being expressed continuously and perpetually in all things. Instead of thinking in terms of cohabitation and human sexual relationships, sex should be thought of as the interchange between pairs of oppositely unbalanced conditions for the purpose of balancing these conditions in every effect of motion in the entire universe. 'Good effects' are those in which the interchange is balanced—and 'bad effects' are those in which balance is not complete."*

*Walter Russell, in his chart of the Periodic Table of the Elements, suggested every element of matter has its polar opposite. For example, sodium and chlorine. He presented to us the idea that sexual difference runs through all things, a Sexual Universe.

Lao Russell (1904-1988)—*Love*, 1966

"Man and woman are forever seeking balanced mates, for they intuitively know that with and through each other they have a greatly multiplied power of expression. The scientific explanation of this multiplied power lies in the fact that not only their bodies but their thinking, also, becomes polarized. This polarization can only come from sex mate-hood between man and woman. That is why homosexuality has a weakening effect rather than a strengthening one. It naturally follows that lesbianism has the same weakening effect. Male and female sex intercourse brings polarization to *balanced* mates. There is a great vitalizing force for both when true love has given birth to the sex desire.

"When a male has sexual relations with another male, or a female with a female, there is not a polarization, but rather a depolarization, which has a *devitalizing* effect. Naturally, the thinking of such people is also unbalanced. In one of our lessons in our *Home Study Course in Universal Law, Natural Science, and Living Philosophy* is the following on POLARITY:

"The basic law of Creation demands equality in all interchange between the pairs of units in all Creation....

"Nature will not tolerate any violation of sex-balance whatsoever and that is why we see anguish, disease, frustrations, divorces, bankruptcies, and many forms of unhappiness around about us everywhere in small scale, and hatreds, enmities, and wars in large scale. All of the troubles of all the world lie in that one cause—breach of the law of polarity which upsets the balance of every transaction between DIVIDED PAIRS.

"When a transaction between divided pairs fails to UNITE those divided pairs, unhappiness is as sure to follow as night follows day. A seesaw is an excellent example of polarity or sex-division. That is why we choose this example. It is important that you realize and recognize that similarity. A seesaw divides the one balance of its fulcrum into two extended balances which must be equally balanced in order to unite and repeat.

"Every interchange is a sex interchange. When a man and woman *talk* together, this is a *mental sex interchange.* Powerful ideas are born of mental sex interchange when a man and woman are *balanced mental mates.* That is why men and women should work together—mentally—because they would then know the ecstasy of balance mental mate-hood.

"Everyone should know the importance of *balanced mating.* A marriage which is based purely upon physical attraction is not a balanced mating. *There must be a spiritual, mental, and physical harmony to fulfill the electrical balance necessary for balanced mate-hood. There* is no law on earth that will hold two people together who do not truly love each other."

"From now on, sex will be regarded in our new perspective as being expressed continuously and perpetually in all things. Instead of thinking in terms of cohabitation and human sexual relationships, sex should be thought of as the interchange between pairs of oppositely unbalanced conditions for the purpose of balancing these conditions in every effect of motion in the entire universe. 'Good effects' are those in which the interchange is balanced—and 'bad effects' are those in which balance is not complete." And that is just the beginning of this paradigm shift. It begins at the spiritual level of things, postulating not just a singular non-creative force but a two **creative** forces, equal and opposite, male and female. There must be this interconnection; a SEXUAL CONNECTION!
We just cannot comprehend a one-force sexless God.

And then there is Walt Whitman, the cosmic poet also postulates a **Sexual Creative Process of Life**. Who would have thought?

Walt Whitman(1819-1892)—Leaves of Grass, 1855
Song for Myself
"I have heard what the talkers were talking....the talk of the beginning and the end,
But I do not talk of the beginning or the end.
There was never any more inception than there is now,
Nor any more youth or age than there is now;
And will never be any more perfection than there is now,
Nor any more heaven or hell than there is now.
Urge and urge and urge,
Always the procreant urge of the world.
Out of the dimness opposite equals advance...Always substance and increase.
Always a knit of identity....always distinction....always a breed of life."

I Sing the Body Electric
"This is the nucleus...after the child is born of woman the

man is born of woman, This is the bath of birth...this is the merge of small and large and the outlet again."

"Urge and urge and urge, Always the procreant urge of the world. Out of the dimness opposite equals advance...." About says it all. If you, or I, don't have *the procreant urge* as our conceptual understanding/beginning point, we have nothing at all.

The Eternal Process of Male and Female Division and Unification

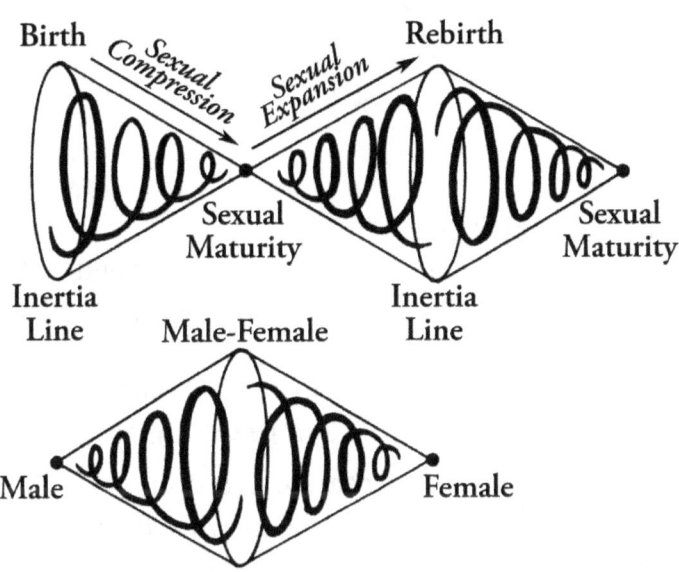

The Universal Axiom of Life

It takes a man and a woman to make a baby!

Richard Garnett (1835-1906)
 "Man and woman may only enter Paradise hand-in-hand. Together…they left it, and together they must return."

O Light Eternal: The Message of Eternal Life from **Selected Writings, Volume 3, A New Trinity © 2024**

The Eternal and the Procreative Are One

The eternal is that which is procreative to life. This will be our message. Our love is a procreative love. Our lives are procreative together. And as such we know the eternal in our hearts and souls as we reach out to each other in the one touch that is an eternal touch. With this said, let me bring to your attention again *The Eternal Prayer. The Eternal Prayer* contains the spirit that comprises the light that is the touch, one sexual soul to another, now and forevermore.

The Eternal Prayer*

My blessed love, please come into my heart and live in me. Allow me, as well, to come into your heat and live in you. Let us, from this moment on, live in each other's hearts, our love together being our guide, shining a light for all to see that life is held simply in our balance together.

***Healing In The Light © 1998**

Spiritual Procreation suggests that the **Procreant Process of Life** does not stop at physical procreation, not even at mental procreation, but encompasses the totality of the physical, mental, and spiritual realms of LIFE. Perhaps it would be better to view what we call "God" as a universal principle of LIFE, consisting of the two universal forces of male and female.
Let There Be Life!

From the poem *Touch, To Cassandra—Early Years* © 1985. The last stanza reads:

> Cassandra
> Shall you and I
> Walk into our silence
> Together
> Down the aisle
> Arm and arm
> Into the abyss
> Forever
> To only return
> When called desire
> Between a man and woman
> To touch.

Our love, that is the love between a man and a woman, is eternal love. Our life together is simply an expression of *our eternal love*. The whole universe of life is an expression of *our eternal love*. Eternal love is eternal life. *Eternal life*, what an interesting idea, brought to consciousness by a simple abstraction between a *one* order and a *two* forces.

Our love is eternal love!

Part 4: Universal Purpose

My purpose: To bring the message of Man and Woman Balance to planet Earth. This was given to me in my late 20's. It came as a light into my consciousness. I was never to be the same.

Later I was to write:

For aeons, mankind has been caught in a trap, a trap so hideous it has prevented men and women from achieving any type of enduring success. Yet, from this trap our religions formed and promised mankind a way out through another world. Later, our socio-political institutions were formed promising us liberation in this world. Yet, neither could deliver, for they were part of the trap, which was nothing but a simple misconception mankind made at the dawn of consciousness preventing him from discovering life.

This was from my writing *The Discovery of Life,* © 1994. The question before us is how do we get to the balance—the understanding that the balance is also our own purpose in life? Let's continue with some further quotes from other writers.

Walter Russell (1871-1963)
"My Purpose and Universal Purpose are One!"

Walter Russell (1871-1963)—*The Divine Iliad*, 1948
"For again I say My one principle of My one law is founded upon the solid rock of equal interchange between all pairs of opposite things, opposite conditions, or opposite transactions between men."

Walt Whitman (1819-1892)—*Leaves of Grass: I Sing the body Electric*, 1855
"This is the nucleus...after the child is born of woman the man is born of woman. This is the bath of birth...this is the merge of small and large and the outlet again."

All creation is really a procreation! This is to say we, male and female, are sexually interconnected. This is the one Order/Law. Order/Law is another term Balance/Purpose. And it is all tied into the two (equal and opposite) eternal forces of male and female. So what, may I ask, is this LGBTQ movement, that is being praised and paraded around, actually about? Might it simply be not a new to life connection but another form of sexual disconnection?

The Two Forces of Creation © 1988—Selected Writings, Volume 2 © 1991, 2010

Male is that force which seeks to individualize form separate and apart from the unity of male-female. The male desire is to hold male and female in individual form. It is the active *conscious* effort of holding separate identity in relationship to the other. The male effort is simply to hold apart and stabilize the man and woman relationship. We call this the effort to secure form or just *security*.

Female is that force which seeks to unite the division of male and female. The female desire is to unite the separate male and female forms together as one. She rests the man and woman relationship through unifying male within herself. It is from this unity that the next division or reproduction can take place. The female effort then is to unite the separate forms of male and female, resting that unity so that the next reproduction of individual form will occur. We call this resting of old form/begetting of new form *reproduction*.

In essence, it is the male effort to secure form and the female effort to reproduce form that makes for life and its continuity. Each aspect makes for one half of the creative process. Yet, and this is an important point, neither aspect can complete their creative desire without the other. The male cannot continually secure form. That effort is fatiguing and brings on a desire to rest. It is at this point that the male takes what he has secured in form and gives it over to female. The male deposits his life seed (force) into the female releasing his form into hers from which his next reproduction will occur. So without periodic rest or release of his form into hers, the male cannot continue to fulfill his own desire to secure form.

Likewise, the female cannot continually rest/reproduce form. She herself must sequentially effort, and does so equal to male in preparing herself to receive male as well as nurturing new form. In this fashion, she supports the securing effort of male. Female is actually called to surrender her life to the male desire to individualize form even though her primary desire is to unite, for without that division of the one into two there would not be the two sexual selves to unite. At this point of unity, the male is called to surrender his life to the female desire to unite the forms even though his primary desire is to individualize. Without the unity of the two into one there would not be a unified one from which male and female could then divide into their sexually unique forms.

It is important to understand the equality of the two different forces of male and female. They each operate under different desires and yet both are equally essential for either of them to be. The male force alone or the female force alone is impotent. Without the other neither can be. They *need* each other. Each is as important to the other as they are to themselves. Both are called upon to make the ultimate surrender of their lives to the other. Neither is ever without the other. Both always are. Male and female, the two forces of creation, are what is. We might just say:

Male, being that force which seeks to individualize a form separate and apart from the unity of male-female.
Female, being that force which seeks to unite separate forms together from the division of male and female.

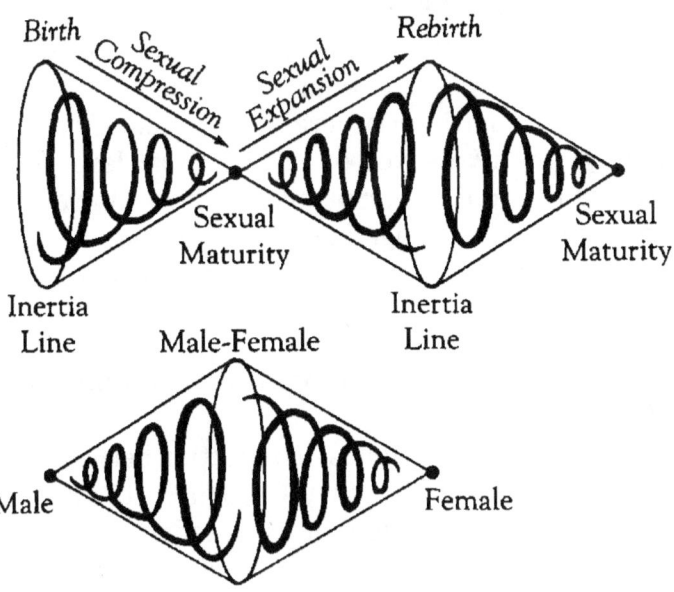

The Discovery of Life © 1994, 2010

We express creation through our sexuality. That is the effort of individual life. Then we release our sexual difference into the unity of rest. In the unification of the two, sexual difference, in that one moment, is voided. The two have become one which is their rest or death. But from that unity comes the next division into sexual difference. This whole process is sexual, creative to life. (I hope it is understood that sexuality is not just physical but metaphysical. It is of the non-beginning and never-ending. It is what is. In other words, we are not beings who just happen to be sexual, we are sexual beings with a sexual purpose.) So, which do you do? Do you divide the one or do you unite the two? This is the great metaphysical question. To answer it, we need to discover our sexual selves, who we are in relation to whom we are not, thereby discovering life. If you are a male, you will do one of these functions. If you are a female, you will do the other. Both functions are equally necessary to life, yet they are opposite. So which are you?

The Metaphysics of Sex …In a Changing World © 2014

On a personal note, when Mr. Anderson was asked to describe the writings and what he felt their message was he responded, "Spiritual procreation. Mankind has yet to distinguish the two sexes on the spiritual level. In this failure lies the root of our problems and why we cannot yet touch the eternal together. The message of Man and Woman Balance brings each of us together in love with our eternal other half right now."

The Eternal Marriage from **Man, Woman, and God © 1994, 2010**

The spiritual connection is a connection between a man and a woman whereby they recognize their eternal creation and love together. It is based in their sexual differentiation from and creative need for each other. In this, a man and woman have *life* purpose together. They are the co-creators of all that is. The formed universe moves through them. They together hold the balance on which all life depends. The world moves one step forward into the light with just one touch of their love.

We Can Only Create Together © 1998

- Man and woman can only create together.
- From the love of a man and a woman new life, a son or a daughter, is born.
- All new born life is divine life.
- Each creation is a divine creation.
- Each creation is the most special creation.
- Each creation is bequeathed with the divine love of Father and Mother.
- Every creation has within its heart the desire to create life with and through its other half.
- Every creation is eternal in its procreative balance with its eternal other half.
- The heartbeat within every creation is the heartbeat of procreative love.
- Procreative love is the life-dynamic of the universe.
- Procreative love is God.
- God is Man and Woman Balance.

- God is expressed when a man and a woman reach out to each other and touch in the one pure, perfect moment of their most special love.
- Only together can a man and a woman create.

This is the e-mail Robert sent to me.

> Chris
> 11/8/99
> "In your writings, you have defined the TRUE nature of the WORD as being PROCREATIVE and the ONE order, context, process, and structure of the universe, and that MAN and WOMAN are its TWO electrodes of manifesting! Without you having made this connection from the Russell's, I wouldn't be writing all this down, and there would be no Ruchell and me, and there would be no "The Secret of Creating the Present Moment." The great awakening would still be floundering, waiting for greater definition. This is the second coming as it were. In the name of Ruchell and me, I PROCLAIM it so."

We can only create together. Do you get it? Everything comes in pairs—even at/on the spiritual level. This is not just physical but mental as well. This is not just mental but spiritual as well. Let us look more deeply into the **Universality of Sexual Creation**.

The Alignment Drawings

```
M — S — F        S             S             S
   |             |             |             |
M — M — F    M — M — F         M             M
   |             |             |             |
M — B — F    M — B — F     M — B — F         B
```

S — Spirit   M — Mind   B — Body   M — Male   F — Female

The Alignment Drawings reveal to us the connection/balance, or lack thereof, of our relationships. This includes our relationships with one another, but also with our environment and our spiritual connections as with "God." Just to review the earlier quote by Walter Russell: *"From now on, sex will be regarded in our new perspective as being expressed continuously and perpetually in all things. Instead of thinking in terms of cohabitation and human sexual relationships, sex should be thought of as the interchange between pairs of oppositely unbalanced conditions for the purpose of balancing these conditions in every effect of motion in the entire universe. 'Good effects' are those in which the interchange is balanced—and 'bad effects' are those in which balance is not complete."*

Moving from left to right, the first drawing shows the balance of equal and opposite occurring on the physical (body), mental, and spiritual levels. The second drawing shows the balance occurring on the physical and mental levels but not on the spiritual level. Then we have the third drawing where the balance is only occurring on the physical level. The fourth drawing reveals a <u>lack of balance</u> on all three levels, the physical, mental, and spiritual. The further one strays from the sexual (equal and opposite) balance the less one will experience a satisfactory life. In fact, one will be causing problems and doing damage to others. And here is where we get to the hard part. *Who wants to admit that their fundamental core belief system is mistaken.* We cling to our own belief system with our very lives. Let me give you an example. We have many religions which, basically, are belief systems: Judaism, Christianity, Islam, Hinduism, Buddhism, etc. I would submit to you that all these religions are not sexually balanced on the spiritual level. They don't make the fundamental metaphysical distinction of God the Father <u>and</u> God the Mother.

This is because they don't view "God" sexually, as a two-force sexual procreant process of life. So how do we get from a one-force "God" to the two sexual forces of male and female? We can't. In result, we place "God" above and before man and woman—and child. But doesn't the Bible state: **Genesis 1:27:** *So God created man in his own image, in the image of God created he him, male and female created he them.* I would suggest to you "God" could not create anything but male and female..., be it human in form as man and woman, or in the basic elements of matter, as in sodium (male) and chlorine (female) as "God" is but a name for the eternal/metaphysical two-force sexually creative process of life. Man and woman together comprise the procreant balance that we call **Life**. "God" is not some non-sexual singular being that somehow creates sexual beings. "God" is but a name for the **Two-Force Sexual Process of Male and Female**. **Genesis 6:19** states: *And of every living thing of all flesh, two of every sort shalt thou bring into the ark, to keep them alive with thee; they shall be male and female.* Why male and female? Could it be because it takes a man and a woman to make a baby, a son or a daughter? Going back to an earlier Russell quote: *"God could not create other than Himself, nor greater, nor lesser than Himself."* Would not this mean that

"God" can only create in male and female pairs? Would not it also mean that the fundamental order/process of all things is but **sexual procreation**? Male and female are not created perse. They comprise the sexual/procreant order of all things. They, the sexes, come together or not at all. God did not create Adam first (Genesis 2:7) and Eve second (Genesis 2:21-23). The sexes are an interlinked creative process—equal and opposite. And the problem we have before us is that we know not that this **Sexual Process of Man and Woman** does also occur at the spiritual level a priori. It, Sexual Procreation, is the **Given of Life.** So instead of *love ye one another* we put "God," or Jesus, etc. before our own husband or wife, or child. We relegate our own husband, wife, or child to second status. Afterall, doesn't one's own eternal life come first? Isn't that what religion is—"My eternal life before yours?" Where is the connection in that? Why? Most likely it is because we consider "our own eternal salvation" to be more important to ourselves than "your eternal salvation." Major mistake! We, and this includes what we call God, are not singular beings/forces. Nothing comes alone. **Everything exists in pairs.** There is no "I Am." There is no "God is." There is only *I Am and You Are.* Listen to this quote from **The Two Forces of Creation**.

The Two Forces of Creation © 1988—Selected Writings, Volume 2 © 1991, 2010

In review, let me suggest that "what is," is relationship-in-process. Relationship-in-process is fundamental or primordial, not a First Cause or One Force. This is to further say that there isn't a supreme being although there may be supreme beings. There isn't a mover of the spheres although there may be movers of the spheres. There isn't a one God who sees all that becomes or forms all immortal beings although there may be gods that do just that.* There is not a single fundamental primordial creative force in the universe, i.e., energy, desire, motive, impulse, purpose, impetus, drive, intention, nature, will, consciousness. Prana, mana, Ki. Chi, Waken, bioplasma, light, cosmic energy, life force, vital pulse, or Holy Spirit. There is only one force in relationship to another force from which creation may then occur. We have to date made a critical mistake in not noting this elementary fact within our conception of order.

*Some language taken from the early Greek philosopher Pythagoras, 570-500 B.C.

"*...a critical mistake in not noting this elementary fact within our conception of order.*" A major mistake. In fact, it is the only mistake. In general, there is no **I Am** without a **You Are**. There is no **Male** without **Female** and vice versa. They come together (equal and opposite) or they do not come at all, i.e., **Force does not and cannot occur without a counter-force.** Perhaps it is time to consider the term "God," if we want to be consistent with creation/order, to consist of a two interconnected Gods—God the Father and God the Mother. You see, you cannot take the sexual aspect of EQUAL and OPPOSITE out of the creation equation. The creation equation is actually a **procreation equation**. The creative balance of all things runs through the Equal and Opposite equation of PROCREATION.

Now, let us look at this next quote, which I take is from Hinduism. Can you see the balance—or the lack there of?

Ervin Laszlo—*Science and the Akashic Field: An Integral Theory of Everything*, 2004
"Although it is undifferentiated, Brahman is dynamic and creative. From its ultimate 'being' comes the temporary 'becoming' of the manifest world, with its attributes, functions, and relationships. The cycles of *samsara*—of being-to-becoming and again of becoming-to-being—are the *lila* of Brahman: its play of ceaseless creation and dissolution. In Indian philosophy, absolute reality is the reality of Brahman. The manifest world enjoys but a derived, secondary reality and mistaking it for the real is the illusion of *maya*. The absolute reality of Brahman and the derived reality of the manifest world constitute a co-created and constantly co-creating whole: this is the *advaitavada* (the non-duality) of the universe."

"The cycles of samsara—of being-to-becoming and again of becoming-to-being—are the lila of Brahman: its play of ceaseless creation and dissolution." Yes, we can see the two-force process in play. That being said, I would not suggest that the manifest world is a "secondary reality." I call it a division of the One into Two, and that it is as **important and primary** as the union of the Two into One. **The two always come together and are equal in necessity to each other.** And, furthermore, that there is a sexual/procreant component in play:

Male, being that force which seeks to individualize a form separate and apart from the unity of male-female.
Female, being that force which seeks to unite separate forms together from the division of male and female.

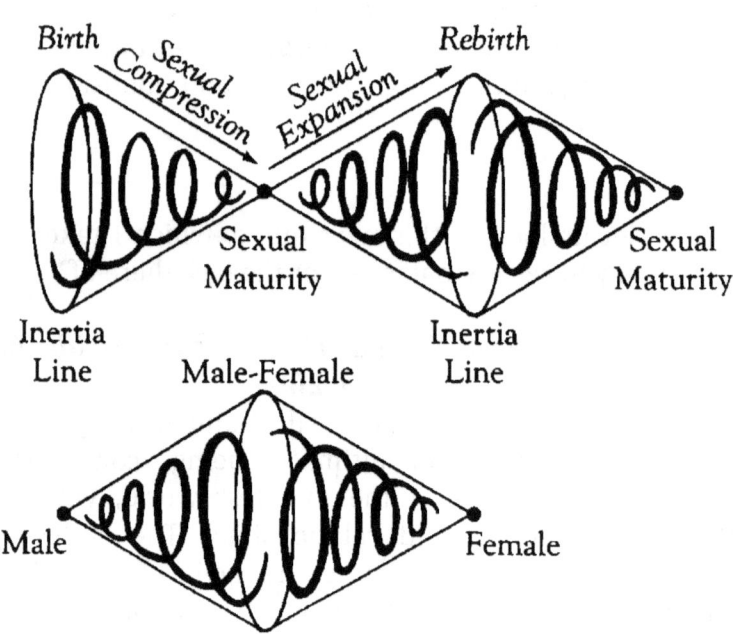

If we don't hold to a balance of the sexual parts we run into the reality of <u>sexual imbalance</u>. For the most part, sexual imbalance has been the controlling force throughout much of our history. We cannot hold our sexual opposite, the other sex, as somehow secondary to us. We must realize when it comes to the sexes: **One is not without the other; both are needed for either to be.** This is the balance point of all things.

There is another critical issue that keeps many glued into the one-force imbalance called "God," and that is the issue of the Virgin Birth. Here it is believed and proclaimed that "God" united with Mary through some type of immaculate conception from which a one and only "Christ Jesus" was born. And furthermore, that without our so believing in this one and only "Son of God" we are doomed to an eternity in hell.

Christ's Virgin Birth (Author Unknown)
"The virgin birth is an underlying assumption in everything the Bible says about Jesus. To throw out the virgin birth is to reject Christ's deity, the accuracy and authority of Scripture, and a host of other related doctrines that are the heart of the Christian faith. No issue is more important than the virgin birth to our understanding of who Jesus is. If we deny that Jesus is God, we have denied the very essence of Christianity. Everything else the Bible teaches about Christ hinges on the truth we celebrate at Christmas—that Jesus is God in human flesh. If the story of His birth is merely a fabricated or trumped-up legend, then so is the rest of what Scripture tells us about Him. The virgin birth is as crucial as the resurrection in substantiating His deity. It is not an optional truth. Anyone who rejects Christ's deity rejects Christ absolutely—even if he pretends otherwise."

Will this belief (in the Virgin Birth) take us to *love ye one another* or does it leave us in a "Me first, You second" positioning? Is it embedded in the two forces, equal and opposite, or just one singular force, believe in me or else?

Structural Balance

Man and Woman Balance

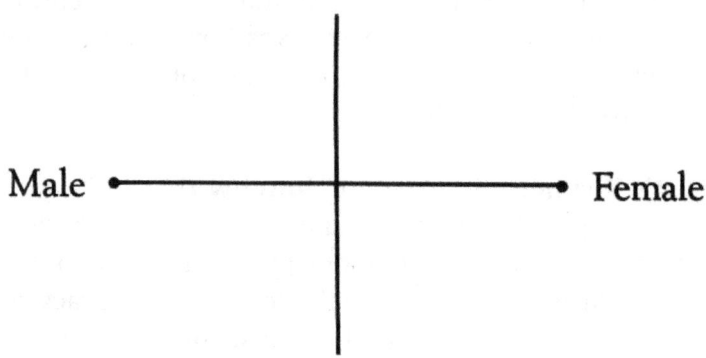

Structural Imbalance

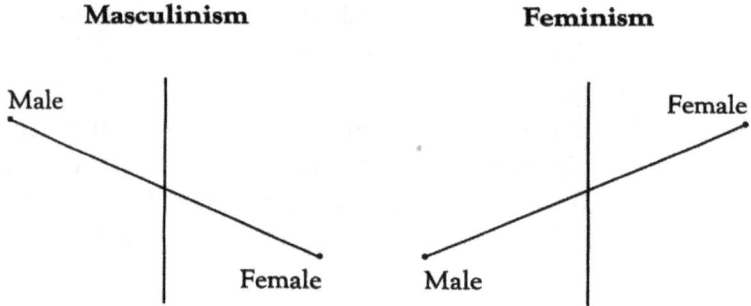

The Three Structures of the Universe

Man and Woman Balance: *Equal and Opposite*
Masculinism: *Opposite but not Equal*
Feminism: *Equal but not Opposite*

The 2008-2009 Articles—Our Purpose Together: Bringing the Eternal Down to Earth © 2010

Neither masculinism nor feminism, in any of its forms, can bring the eternal down to earth. This is now for us (man and woman pairs) to do. It is *our purpose* to touch in love *together* and, by doing so, we, man and woman, bring the eternal down to earth. We do this by living *our love* in our lives. The eternal is always a procreant balance between metaphysical primaries or duals. There isn't anything more sacred, in the light, or of eternal life than that one procreant touch between one man and one woman right now. That one touch will last forever when you know it.

Wealth Plus⁺ Empowering Your Everyday! © 2013

The perfection of the soul can only be found in sexual union.

We cannot take the sexual out of metaphysical or physical life and hope to survive. It is through the sexual domain of male and female that the opposite two can unite as one. And then from this unity the next division, a new life, can be brought forth. There isn't any other reality in life. All these other supposedly "transcendent realities" to sexual life and love are illusions of life. They are not real. They cannot exist. You can't find life, love, or children there. What you do find is a poverty consciousness. The reason why Wealth Plus⁺ stands on the procreant process as the center of all existence is because wealth, primordially, can only be found in the balance and love between a man and a woman. That is its center point from which all things radiate. That is its point of perfection.

Your only universal purpose is to give and receive love.

To give and receive love is the basis of balance. If we are taking from another, blaming another, bad-mouthing another, not keeping our agreements with another, being unfaithful to another, forcing another, etc., we are out of balance with him or her. At that moment the balance of love is lost. At that moment we enter into poverty consciousness (lack-blame-demand-attack). At that moment, as per the Law of Balance, we lose our wealth. You see, at the very center of all life is one simple interaction one to another, and that is the giving and receiving of love. If we do not begin from there how can we ever be wealthy? Wealth first begins as a <u>wealth in spirit</u>.

"God" is never supernatural; "God" is only personal.

The balance of procreant love between a man and a woman is as personal as things get. To somehow transcend this love into some "sexless realm," as if there can be some sexless realm, is the height of not just ignorance but arrogance. <u>There is no greater love than your love right now as you are giving it to another. Likewise, there is no greater act of love than in receiving the love given to you by another.</u> Each one of us is wealthy with love right now as we give to and receive from our sexual other half. We need not look any further. And, as I have said, if you are not physically with your love's calling right now, please know, you always are together spiritually.

So, a decision is at hand. Can you make the shift from God the Father to God the Father <u>and</u> God the Mother?

If there be a "God the Father" there must also be a
"God the Mother," not a "God the Mother" as a secondary existence to "God the Father," but and an
equal and opposite primary existence to "God the Father."

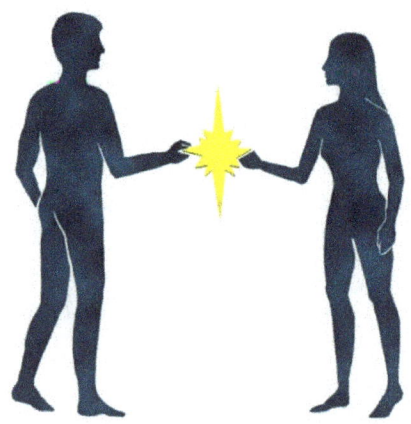

My view of Jesus* is that he was not born via a Virgin Birth, but that he was an empath. This is to suggest that his heart was open. He could feel the hopes and hurts of others. He healed by taking on those very hopes and hurts. **Mark 5:30, 34:** "...*Who touched my clothes? ...Daughter, thy faith hath made the whole; go in peace, and be whole of thy plague.*" From this spiritual healing comes both mental and physical healing. This is to suggest that Jesus understood the spiritual balance/interconnection of all things. Let us not believe in Jesus; let us have the heart of Jesus. If we could just do that much.

*Some suggest Jesus was an Essene and was married to Mary Magdalene. Will we ever know?

Franz Hartmann, M.D. (1838-1912)—*The Life of Jehoshua, The Prophet of Nazareth*, 1888

""*The Christ*' or '*Messiah*,' means the redeeming power of *Universal* spiritual consciousness, love, and intelligence, while the limited 'Christ' of the churches is merely a person, whose love manifests itself at best inside the church. The real Christ means *Universal Life*, while the 'Christ' of the sects means separateness and favouritism."

"In '*Jesus of Nazareth*' we behold a beautiful allegory, representing the spiritual germ of divine Intelligence in the soul of Man, conceived in the heart by the power of the spirit of Divine Wisdom, continually born in the mystic *Bethlehem* situated in the purest region of the human soul. To speak of Him as an 'historical person' is a blasphemy and an absurdity. He never was killed by the Jews, although he is continually crucified by professed Christians. He is alive to-day and will live forever, and resides in the hearts of those who adore him and obey his commands."

I had not heard of Franz Hartmann until recently. Check out his collection of writings if you will. Amazing. I think he may concur with this statement, **"The measure of your love is dependent not on what you believe nor on the size of your giving but on the purity of your heart."**

Let us return to the Alignment Drawings.

The Alignment Drawings

```
M — S — F        S             S            S
   |             |             |            |
M — M — F    M — M — F         M            M
   |             |             |            |
M — B — F    M — B — F     M — B — F        B
```

S — Spirit   M — Mind   B — Body   M — Male   F — Female

We have covered the first two drawings. The first one makes the sexual distinction of male as to female on all three levels, Spirit, Mind, and Body. As such there is a Balance of Life in play Spiritually, Mentally, and Physically. The second one only makes the sexual distinction on the Mental and Physical levels. On the Spiritual level the two sexes are not really differentiated and thus there is a loss of Spiritual Balance. We might say there is a collapse into Oneness (Unity) without the equal necessity of Twoness (Division), i.e., no Sexual/Life distinction on the Spiritual level. And so we have various "religions" claiming "My God is the only God!"

The third drawing shows a collapse on both the mental and spiritual levels. What might this be and how does it affect us? Let us see.

"The Communists disdain to conceal their views and aims. They openly declare that their ends can be attained only by the forcible overthrow of all existing social conditions. Let the ruling classes tremble at a Communistic revolution. The proletarians have nothing to lose but their chains. They have a world to win.
"Working Men of all Countries, Unite!"*

Manifesto of the Communist Party by Karl Marx and Frederick Engels, 1848

The Man and Woman Manifesto: What We Believe! © 2017

Thus ends one of the most prophetic declarations from one of the most profound and influential books ever written. This, of course, is *The Communist Manifesto* (more formally called *Manifesto of the Communist Party*) by Karl Marx and Frederick Engels, 1848. Why do I begin this writing with a quote from Marx and Engels? Because, at least in my view, it seems we are on the verge of another ideology of class struggle/warfare. Not that the class struggle (between the Haves and the Have-nots) has ever gone away but that its *ideology* and *cause* is resurfacing, perhaps under different labels, to be used as justification for one or more people to use that deadly instrument of *forcible overthrow* to acquire their desires and needs. By forcible overthrow I mean violence—*the use of force one upon another*—and, of course, its justification. This issue of violence (force) has yet to be resolved.

Today we have the same revolution going on, perhaps under and different name. Whatever name we call it: Socialism, Democracy, Statism, Collectivism, Liberalism, Corporate Fascism, Federalism, the Military Industrial Complex, etc., it basically breaks down into central control/authority and your life and property being held, by force if necessary, in the hands of the elite/state. I often refer to this despotism as the Nation State, or just the Deep State; those embedded <u>politicians</u> and/or <u>bureaucrats</u> that never seem to go away. They, more or less, have a monopoly on the use of force and the use/control of money/property. Now, you might be wondering, what does the third alignment drawing have to do Socialism, etc.? You may be thinking, "So one doesn't hold to the belief of a two (equal and opposite) forces on the spiritual and mental levels of life? So what! Who knows if a balance exists at all!" Good questions. In the case of Socialism, as per the Alignment Drawings, there is an imbalance occurring on two of the three levels. This is to say that Socialism, essentially government by force, is two-thirds imbalanced. Have you ever wondered why socialistic countries can never seem to produce enough for their basic needs? The Austrian economist Ludwig von Mises (1881-1973) put it this way in his writing *Socialism,* 1922:

Socialism, 1922

"Everything brought forward in favor of socialism during the last hundred years, in thousands of writings and speeches, all the blood which has been spilt by the supporters of socialism, cannot make socialism workable."

Powerful quote! Why would this be the case? It is simple, under socialism you, and I, are not free. This is to say we do not have unalienable rights; we are not co-sovereigns. We do not get to pursue our dreams (effort) nor keep the fruits of our labor (ownership). Somebody else is telling us what to do. And our individual *initiative* (hopes and dreams) and thus *ingenuity* dies. Following are three other von Mises quotes followed by quotes from others. Most of the quotes are critical of socialism/fascism and rightly so. A few are by "thinkers" who actually favor top-down government. Sprinkled in are some quotes favoring a Constitutional Republic. I use the term Constitutional Republic as that system of governance based in the **Sovereignty** of each and every one of us, i.e., that we, You and I, by the nature and right of our lives hold **Unalienable Rights—*the rights of life, liberty, and ownership of our labor/productivity*.** Again, from von Mises.

Human Action, 1949
"Every socialist is a disguised dictator."

Planning for Freedom, 1952
"Under socialism production is entirely directed by the orders of the central board of production management. The whole nation is an 'industrial army' ...and each citizen is bound to obey his superior's orders."

Bureaucracy, 1944
"In the bureaucratic machine of socialism the way toward promotion is not achievement but the favor of the superiors."

John Adams (1735-1826), 2nd American President
"Liberty once lost is lost forever. When the People once surrender their share in the Legislature, and their Right of defending the Limitations upon the government, and of

resisting every Encroachment upon them, they can never regain it."

"All the perplexities, confusion and distress in America arise, not form defects in their constitution or confederation, not from want of honor or virtue, so much as from the downright ignorance of the nature of coin, credit and circulation."

Arnold Ahlert—columnist

"Scholarly debate about its various clauses has been non-stop since the document became the law of the land. But one aspect of the Constitution is beyond debate: it is a document entirely constructed to limit the power of the *government*, not the people."

President Calvin Coolidge (1872-1933), 30th American President

"I want the people of America to be able to work less for the government and more for themselves. I want them to have the rewards of their own industry. This is the chief meaning of freedom. Until we can re-establish a condition under which the earnings of the people can be kept by the people, we are bound to suffer a very severe and distinct curtailment of our liberty."

Frederic Bastiat (1801-1850), French economist, statesman and author

"Government is the great fiction through which everybody endeavors to live at the expense of everyone else."

"Everyone wants to live at the expense of the state. They forget that the state lives at the expense of everyone."

"But how is this legal plunder to be identified? Quite simply. See if the law takes from some persons what belongs to them, and gives it to other persons to whom it does not belong. See if the law benefits one citizen at the expense of another by doing what the citizen himself cannot do without committing a crime."

Ernest Benn (1875-1954), British publisher and writer

"Politics is the art of looking for trouble, finding it whether it exists or not, diagnosing it incorrectly, and applying the wrong remedy."

H. L. Birum, Sr., *American Mercury*, August 1957

"The Federal Reserve Banking is nothing but a banking fraud and an unlawful crime against Civilization. Why? Because they "create" the money made out of nothing, and our Uncle Sap Government issues their "Federal Reserve Notes" and stamps our Government approval with NO obligation whatever from these Federal Reserve Banks, Individual Banks or National Banks, etc."

Jack Crooks—*The Money Trader*

"I pledge allegiance, to the flag, of the United Currency of the World, and to the International Monetary Fund, for which it stands, one Money, more powerful than dollars, indivisible, stealing economic advantages and liberty from all."

James Dale Davidson—*Strategic Investment*

"As you write out your check to the IRS, consider this: In the last 20 years, American politicians have spent $4,000,000,000,000 they didn't have. They have impoverished our nation, and you and your descendants are going to pay the price for decades."

Ralph Waldo Emerson (1803-1882), American writer/philosopher

"A dollar is not value, but representative of value, and, of last, of moral value."

Ayn Rand (1905-1982)—*Atlas Shrugged*, Author and Philosopher, 1957

"When you see that trading is done, not by consent, but by compulsion—when you see that in order to produce, you need to obtain permission from men who produce nothing—when you see money flowing to those who deal, not in goods, but in favors—when you see that men get richer by graft and pull than by work, and your laws don't protect you against them but protect them against you—when you see corruption being rewarded and honesty becoming a self-sacrifice—you may know that your society is doomed."

Ronald Reagan (1911-2004), 40th President of the United States

"I just wanted to speak to you about something from the Internal Revenue Code. It is the last sentence of section 509A of the code and it reads: 'For purposes of paragraph 3, an organization described in paragraph 2 shall be deemed to include an organization described in section 501C-4,5, or 6, which would be described in paragraph 2 if it were an organization described in section 501C-3.' And that's just one sentence out of those fifty-seven feet of books."

Fyodor Dostoyevsky (1821-1881), Russian writer

"The problem of Communism is not an economic problem. The problem of Communism is the problem of atheism."

Fifth Amendment of the Constitution of the United States

"No person shall be deprived of life, liberty, or property, without due process of law."

Milton Friedman (1912-2006), American economist

"Nothing is so permanent as a temporary government program."

"Underlying most arguments against the free market is a lack of belief in freedom itself."

"Concentrated power is not rendered harmless by the good intentions of those who create it."

"Governments never learn. Only people learn.

"Inflation is taxation without legislation."

"Inflation is the one form of taxation that can be

imposed without legislation.

"Is it really true that political self-interest is nobler somehow than economic self-interest?"

"Nothing is so permanent as a temporary government program."

James A. Garfield (1831-1881), 20th American President

"Whoever controls the volume of money in any country is absolute master of all industry and commerce."

Senator Carter Glass, June 7, 1938

"I had never thought the Federal Bank System would prove such a failure. The country is in a state of irretrievable bankruptcy."

Johann Wolfgang von Goethe (1749-1832)

"None are more hopelessly enslaved then those who falsely believe they are free."

Thomas Jefferson (1743-1826), 3rd American President

"If the American people ever allow private banks to control the issue of their currency, first by inflation, then by deflation, the banks....will deprive the people of all property until their children wakeup homeless on the continent their fathers conquered....The issuing power should be taken from the banks and restored to the people, to whom it properly belongs."

Merrill M.E. Jenkins Sr.—*"Money" The Greatest Hoax on Earth*, 1971

"Dollar: Formerly a name to describe a temporarily fixed amount of gold.

Dollar: today: An expression of measure to facilitate cross reference between wealth and money (credit) (inflation), for the purpose of expropriation of the people's wealth without their knowledge."

Income Tax—Voluntary? (Author unknown)
"Yes, in answer to your question; the income tax system is voluntary and we will put every free American in prison to enhance voluntary compliance."

Ferdinand Lassalle—Founder of the German Socialist Movement
"The state is God."

James Madison (1751-1836)—Founding Father and 4th United States President
"If Congress can do whatever in their discretion can be done by money, and will promote the General Welfare, the Government is no longer a limited one, possessing enumerated powers, but an indefinite one...."

Norman Mailer (1923-2007)—American writer
"The function of socialism is to raise suffering to a higher level."

Karl Marx (1818-1884)—*Critique of the Gotha Program*
"From each according to his abilities, to each according to his needs."

Karl Marx and Frederick Engels—*Manifesto of the Communist Party*, 1848
"The Communists disdain to conceal their views and aims. They openly declare that their ends can be attained only by the forcible overthrow of all existing social conditions. Let the ruling classes tremble at a Communistic revolution. The proletarians have nothing to lose but their chains. They have a world to win. Workers of the world, Unite!"

Eustace Mullins (1923-2010)—*The Secrets of the Federal Reserve*
"The 'National Debt' is nothing more than the interest charged the United States by the Federal Reserve on money it created out of nothing."

Friedrich Nietzsche (1844-1900)—*The New Idol, Thus Spoke Zarathustra, 1883*

"The state? What is that, then? Open your ears, and I will speak to you about the death of peoples."

"The state is the coldest monster of all. It lies coldly; and this is the coldest lie that slithers out of its mouth: I, the state, am the people.'"

George Orwell (1903-1950)—*1984*

"If you want a picture of the future, imagine a boot stomping on a human face--forever."

"In a time of deceit, telling the truth is a revolutionary act."

"Political language -- and with variations this is true of all political parties, from Conservatives to Anarchists -- is designed to make lies sound truthful and murder respectable."

"Every record has been destroyed or falsified, every book rewritten, every picture has been repainted, every statue and street building has been renamed, every date has been altered. And the process is continuing day by day and minute by minute. History has stopped. Nothing exists except an endless present in which the Party is always right."

"The Party seeks power entirely for its own sake. We are not interested in the good of others; we are interested solely in power. Not wealth or luxury or long life or happiness: only power, pure power. ... We know that no one ever seizes power with the intention of relinquishing it. Power is not a means, it is an end. One does not establish a dictatorship in order to safeguard a revolution; one makes the revolution in order to establish the dictatorship. The object of persecution is persecution. The object of torture is torture. The object of power is power. Now do you begin to understand me?"

"Now do you begin to understand me?" Powerful words! Right now, we have a socialist running for president in the USA. We may hear the words or something like them, "I am not a socialist; I believe in democracy." I would suggest that is pretty much the same thing today. Look at the Communist Party (CPUSA) website. They believe in socialism. They believe in democracy. They believe in progressivism. They believe in social justice. The one thing they don't believe in is individual/unalienable rights. They don't believe You and I are the SOVEREIGN! WE THE PEOPLE! The point to all this is that unalienable rights can never be separate from *your* earning and owing. This is what it means to say that unalienable rights really constitute property rights.

The Unalienable Rights Test*

- *A right must be based in individual life.*
- *A right must be the same for everyone.*
- *A right can never be taken away.*
- *A right can never be a (consumptive) need.*
- *A right can never circumvent the right of another.*

* *What Ever Happened to Our Unalienable Rights* © 1998, Christopher Alan Anderson

Let's continue this great quote and followed by some diagrams from my writings. This may help in clearing up some questions.

The Declaration of Independence, 1776

"We hold these Truths to be self-evident, that all Men are created equal, that they are endowed by their Creator with certain unalienable Rights, that among these are Life, Liberty, and the pursuit of Happiness—That to secure these Rights, Governments are instituted among Men, deriving their just Powers from the Consent of the Governed, that whenever any Form of Government becomes destructive of these Ends, it is the Right of the People to alter or to abolish it...."

Model of Freedom

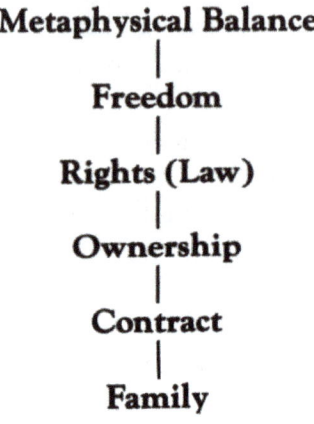

Metaphysical Balance
|
Freedom
|
Rights (Law)
|
Ownership
|
Contract
|
Family

The Nation-State

- *Promises you success within it.*
- *Wants you dependent on it.*
- *Forces you to pay into it.*
- *Gives you the vote to believe it.*
- *Prevents you from leaving it.*

Economic Freedom

The right to earn, keep, and spend as one chooses.

Coercion

One man's use, or threat, of force upon another.

The Purpose of Coercion

Thievery: One's taking of value from another without that other's consent.

The Forced Exchange

Something-for-Nothing Transaction based on one party's coercion another.

The Free Exchange

Something-for-Something Transaction based on the parties' mutual consent upon

The Third-Force Model of Thievery

State (Individual C)

Individual A (Producer)   Individual B (Consumer)

C takes from A and gives to B while keeping 90% of it for itself.

Methods of Allocating Ownership

Ownership by earning (right)---A free exchange.
Ownership by might—A coercive exchange.
Ownership by need—A coercive exchange.

The Parameter of Charity

- ❖ *No one shall be forced to help another.*
- ❖ *No one shall be prevented from helping another.*
- ❖ *No one shall be forced to receive the help of another.*
- ❖ *No one shall be prevented from receiving the help of another.*

Prosperity

Freedom + Productive Effort = Prosperity

The Law of Proportionality

The size of government is inversely proportional to the wealth of the people!

Let us understand, today we are in a financial world war. The "good guys," who we have believed in, turned out not to be so good. They have continued to live outside of their means, to continually raise taxes and regulations while not balancing their own budgets/expenditures. We, here in the "USA corporation," are some 35 trillion in debt. How is that to work? What backs the dollar? Where is the gold? Who owns all the property? What is the military industrial complex? Why is there an IRS? Or CIA? Are **we the people** just surfs? Why do the politicians get to decide what their perks, pensions, and health care plans will be? Why are corporations in bed with politicians? How about some term limits, not just for the politicians but for all bureaucrats—and their agencies—as well? How about some school choice, and medical choice too? And how about an election where only citizens can vote or donate to a politician's campaign? Having a secure boarder would be nice too. Have **We the People** forgotten that government is created to serve us? We the People are the **sovereign**. Sovereignty is another word for **balance**. Rhythmic Balance Interchange. *I Am and You Are!* The balance (on all three levels) must be absolute for our unalienable rights to carry us through.

Confessions of an "Honest" Politician

- Though I speak with the fluidness of the well-educated, and most certainly have your best interests in mind, ...if I do not allow you to keep what you earn, I am just another thug on the take.

- Though I speak of your "human rights" ...if I claim your rights actually originate from me, the government, it is just because I want the right over your pocketbook!

- Though I speak of "tax fairness" ...if I legislate a progressive (income tax) upon you, it is because I am just trying to control your bank account!

- Though I speak of helping the middle class ...if I give subsidies/favors to business or union interests, I am just trying to get my hands on your wallet!

- Though I speak of job creation ...if I demand you get a "business license" to work (and call your work a "profession"), I just want your money!

- Though I speak of justice for all ...if I pass laws that I myself do not have to adhere to, I am just trying to steal your stuff!

- Though I speak of fiscal responsibility ...if I pass budgets that are not balanced, I only want you to pay my way!

- Though I speak of openness and transparency ...if I vote on legislation that has yet to be read by me, I am just trying to hide from you its cost to you!

- Though I speak of income fairness …if I give myself the power to decide what my own salary, perks, and pension will be, I just want you to know that there really are two classes of people!

- Though I speak of governmental accountability …if I approve a governmental accountability review board to be run by government (paid, perked, and pensioned) bureaucrats, it is just me doing my job of holding sovereignty over you!

- Though I speak of freedom, and liberty and justice for all …I still just want your money!

Copyright © 2013 Christopher Alan Anderson

One of the great surprises now coming to the surface in many people is the discovery that most of what we have been told/taught, through our religious or political arenas, the medical and educational institutions, through the media… even in our elections* is a fraud, a cover-up of the truth, and a spreading of an agenda that benefits certain people at the expense of others. How many people today really understand the importance of unalienable rights, "We hold these truths self-evident…" or The Bill of Rights? Our government hasn't served us for a long time. We serve them. Take that in. Its decision time!

*As I am writing this our perhaps most important election in our history is but a few days away.

Whittaker Chambers (1901-1961)—Witness, 1952

"One thing I knew: I was no longer a Communist. I had broken involuntarily with Communism at the moment when I first said to myself: 'It is just as evil to kill the Tsar and his family and throw their bodies down a mine shaft as it is to starve two million peasants or slave laborers to death. More bodies are involved in one case than the other. But one is just as evil as the other, not more evil, not less evil.' I do not know at just what point I said this. I did not even know that with that thought I had rejected the right of the mind to justify evil in the name of history, reason or progress, because I had asserted that there is something greater than the mind, history, or progress. I did not know that this Something is God."

The Man and Woman Manifesto: Let the Revolution Begin © 1994, 2010

...I have come to realize that I no longer believe in the United States of America. I do not believe that the United States any longer stands for freedom and, as structured today, is incompatible with freedom. For me, I no longer view myself to be a "citizen" of this country, or of any country, but rather just a man who is part of the universal ***Community of Man and Woman.***

Can you make the break? Not necessarily from just Communism but from any form of fascism. You can claim you are for the people all you want but that will never make Communism work. Why? Because someone else, elected or not, is telling you how you will live your life. If you want to live on a commune, fine. But don't tell others they must live on a commune, or they can't own property, or that they must pay "income taxes." Now we have another form of fascism emerging with the Diversity, Equity, and Inclusion agenda? Well, how about LGBTQ in total? If you are still with me, let us turn to the last Alignment Drawing. In this case the sexual distinction is not being made on any of the levels—spiritual, mental, or physical. Basically, what this does is cut out the family unit. The sexual process is the family process. Procreation is about the continuation/lineage of life. Without the man and woman distinction (equal and opposite) being made on all three levels, life is precarious at best. Essentially, there isn't the procreation of life, at least not in its spiritual fullness. So, ask yourself, what is going to happen if we don't make the sexual distinction on all (or any) of these levels?

The Alignment Drawings

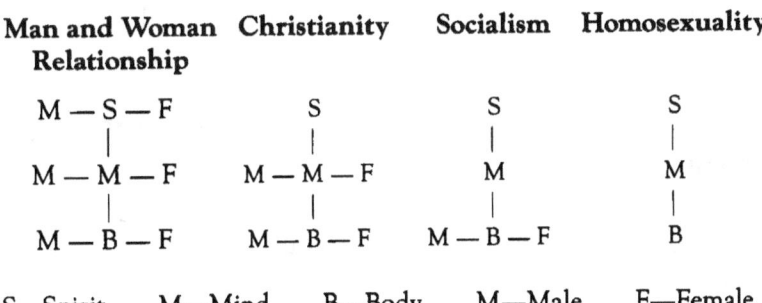

The Man and Woman Manifesto: Let the Revolution Begin © 1985, 2010 The Sovereignty of the Family

Family is the sovereign unit of all creation. It stands at the hub or center of life. It is the source of all things. A family is, by definition, composed of a male and a female. The two equal but opposite forces are in play, dividing and uniting together. From each unity of a male and a female comes procreation, a *reproduction of life.* Family is the most essential thing in all of life. It is life.

Max Freedom Long (1890-1971)—*What Jesus Taught in Secret*, 1983

"It is the Father-Mother who is appealed to in prayer and on whose 'name' we must call."

Emanuel Swedenborg (1688-1772)—*The Sensible Joy in Married Love and The Foolish Pleasures of Illicit Love*, 1768

"The principle of marriage is like the balance in which that love is weighed. For the marriage principle of one man with one wife is the precious treasure of human life and the treasure of the Christian religion. And because it is like this, that love can be found in one marriage and at the same time not in another. And that love can lie too deeply hidden for the person himself to notice it at all. And also, it can be inscribed as his life goes on. The reason is that that love goes in step with religion, and religion is the marriage of the Lord and the church, so it initiates and implants that love. So married love is attributed to someone after death according to the rational life of his spirit. And one whom that love is implanted in is provided a marriage in heaven after death, whatever kind of marriage he had in the world."

The Universal Religion: The Final Destiny of Mankind © 1994

A child is born represents the touch of love (balance) between a man and a woman. That one touch is the whole foundation of the universe. It is a direct touch, a complete touch. It is the touch of life. All that is required for this touch is a man and a woman, conscious of their creativity (connection) together. In their consciousness of life, they touch and—a child is born. This touch is the truth of life. There isn't any greater truth than life. In the universal religion, only the two forces exist expressing their love and their life. There isn't anything else but a male and a female in creative balance. Nothing else is recognized for nothing else exists. This perfect state of creative balance is known as God. Why? Because from this balance a child can be born.

The family unit is under assault. You might be asking yourself, "How can this be?" Good question. After all, without the procreant (male and female) family unit life will not exist. I wonder, what is the psychology/neurology of those who seemingly want to alter if not replace the family unit?

Psychotherapy As If Life Really Mattered © 1995

Today some people are choosing their same sex, a homosexuality. But nowhere have we metaphysically chosen our own (equal and opposite) other half. Since the beginning of it all, we have failed to choose each other. Think about it. To date, we have all made the wrong choice. Recognize it. Acknowledge that you, too, have chosen everything but your equal and opposite other half. Feel it. Scream...

The Psychotic Scream

I have chosen everything but you!

Psychotherapy As If Life Really Mattered © 1995

There is only one choice in life—each (equal and opposite) other. In the one-force paradigm, this is the exact choice we have not been able to spiritually make. No wonder why we long ago went crazy. We are blocked from our procreative life together in spirit, mind, and body. But with the understanding of the two forces of creation in making the conscious metaphysical distinction between male and female, we can now rectify this problem. We can accept our other half into our hearts and lives by simply saying, *"I choose you."* Such is the existential choice that will bring life to our lives.

The Existential Choice

Man—*I choose you, woman.*

Woman—*I choose you, man.*

"*I choose you*" is the choice to *live.* Without this *conscious* choice, we stay trapped in the (one-force) imbalance and never know true love. The imbalance of hate will take love's place and will surface in one of two ways. In one way, the focus is on the opposition of the sexual two at the denial of their equality. This imbalance is known as *masculinism*. In the other case, the focus is on their equality at the expense of their opposition. This imbalance is known as *feminism*. In both masculinism and feminism, sexual/spiritual (procreative) *touch* just cannot take place and, to that degree, life itself is thwarted. The spirit of the man or woman dies, even though one may try and rally the forces for the cause one more time.

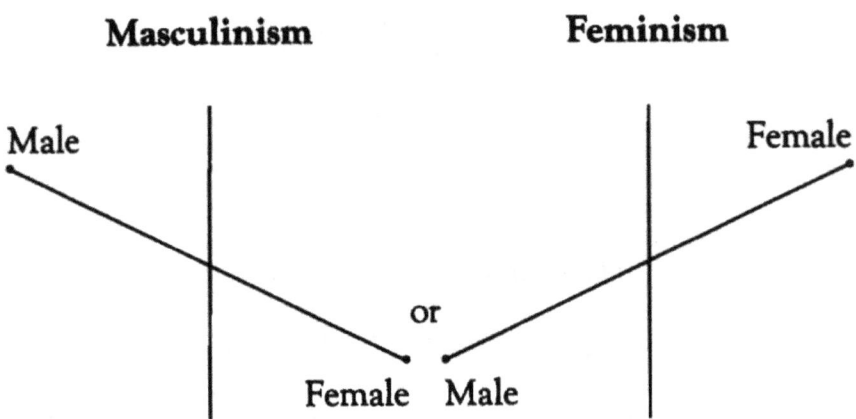

Psychotherapy As If Life Really Mattered © 1995

The extreme form of masculinism or feminism surfaces in what is known as homosexuality. In homosexuality, one is essentially saying to his or her opposite other half, "I don't want you or need you." Unfortunately, this is not true. We all need that other half. Both male and female are required for *life.* Without both male *and* female, procreation (security/reproduction) stops. Has anyone ever noticed that it takes both a man and a woman to make a baby? Metaphysically speaking, two men together cannot unite the two and two women together cannot divide the one. This is a metaphysical fact. *We just are not able to "transcend" the (equal but opposite) structure of the universe.* Without both forces (sexes), this universe would simply be a lifeless void. Remember that the next time you join in or cheer the gay and lesbian "liberation/pride parade." These people are actually parading for their death, *and they want to include you, too!*

"But, isn't love, love?" you ask. We hear this all the time. "Anyway, what business is this your yours? Who are you to tell consenting adults what their sexual decisions will be?" My answer is simple. Homosexuality, or shall we call it LGBTQ today, is not a sexual action. There isn't any procreative potentiality. There must be that connection. Even in elderly couples, the spiritual sense of procreation is present. I mean, are you really saying that sodomy, for example, has anything to do with the procreation of life? Sodomy, and like things, is not and can never be an act of love. In fact, "anal sex" is not, and can never be, sexual union. (Two men cannot Unite the Two!) The use of dildos and the like can never bring on new life. (Two woman cannot Divide the One!) Or what about the Trans movement—even for children? One cannot change his or her sexuality. It's a metaphysical Given. Men can't get pregnant. And woman don't carry the male seed. We are walking the line of insanity here. And what about pedophilia? Those involved in that activity have crossed the line, in many cases killing the spirits, and perhaps the body too, of a boy or girl. May I suggest that what "love is love" really means is that anything goes, even, if I am hearing correctly, sex trafficking and sacrifice. For the LGBTQ crowd there is no line to be drawn in the sand. Yet, notice how the LGBTQ movement wants (and even demands) to be able to partake in having access to children, through adoption or using a surrogate or in vitro fertilization, etc., even though their whole advocacy precludes the procreation of life. No, you don't get to be with the children as your own actions preclude the reality of procreation, i.e., love.

Sigmund Freud (1856-1939)—*The Sexual Life of Human Beings,* 1920

"The abandonment of the reproductive function is the common feature of all perversions. We actually describe a sexual activity as perverse if it has given up the aim of reproduction and pursues the attainment of pleasure as an aim independent of it. So, as you will see, the reach and turning point in the development of sexual life lies in becoming subordinate to the purpose of reproduction.

Everything that happens before this turn of events and equally everything that disregards it and that aims solely at obtaining pleasure is given the uncomplimentary name of "perverse" and as such is proscribed."

Don Feder—columnist

"Surrender on gay marriage is surrender on marriage—which is surrender on the family and, ultimately, surrender on civilization. ... This unwillingness to fight for the family, on which civilization depends, is another sign of the failure of modern conservatism. The right can win a thousand battles against big government and lose the war for America's future, if it surrenders on marriage and the family. America's social traumas—illegitimacy, juvenile crime, drug abuse, female-headed-households—can all be traced back to the decline of the family: which started with the Great Society in the '60s, accelerated with no-fault divorce in the '70s, continued with the rise of cohabitation, and reached its culmination with same-sex marriage. ... Unfortunately, many conservative intellectuals have lost sight of a crucial fact: American exceptionalism rests on three pillars—faith, family and freedom. Remove any one, and the entire structure collapses. ... Without the family, it doesn't matter how many times we defeat socialism (nationalized health-care, government take-over of business, soaring deficits, redistributionism), in the end, we lose—which is why the left has made same-sex marriage its priority, and why it is less tolerant of dissent here than anywhere else. Conservatives who don't understand this, understand nothing."

Psychotherapy As If Life Really Mattered © 1995

The homosexual "attraction" or "choice" is not for one's own sex as most think. The initial choice was (and is) to be unconscious (of reality). Somewhere in time, one had an experience that he or she perceived they had no control over and they, out of fear/survival, went unconscious. This imbalance later surfaces as an unconscious attraction for imbalance. This is the form or basis of any addiction. To cure this imbalance one has to go back into his or her psyche and *consciously* experience that moment of unconsciousness or imbalance. Of course, one cannot do this without first knowing the creative balance. In *procreant* balance (creative nature), homosexuality does not exist. It is simply a reflection of the unconscious/sexual imbalance we hold. As man and woman balance is brought into light, homosexuality, and all imbalances, will disappear. But let us never mistake the non-procreative nature of homosexuality. It does not make the sexual (creative) distinction on any level, spiritual, mental, or physical. That is its problem and its danger.

We might include abortion in this discussion as well. Abortion, at it's best, must be the last choice and only considered in the narrow parameter of rape, incest, or the health of the mother or child. I don't mean mental health but physical health. Is the mother's life at stake? Does the child have a severe physical deformity? We cannot allow abortion for convenience. We hear of some people demanding abortion on demand for any reason they may have all the way up to the birth of the child—and maybe even after the birth of the child! How can this be? Perhaps one should seriously consider the ramifications of the sexual act? It is a **sacred** act. Its measure is love. Its outcome is life, a new born son or daughter. We should not be having sex without love and commitment. This is what a marriage is all about. The Two become as One become as Three. Marriage is what holds a family unit together. It is its **procreant** frame. And all we do is complain because we can't afford "protection" or can't get an "abortion on demand." Now, I am not suggesting a couple should not share intimacy together. That is what romance and love is all about. But let's go to first base first, and then second and third base, before we touch home plate. And let's also have some commitment going in, maybe even marriage. Wow, what a novel idea! We just cannot have our cake and eat it too. Life is at issue and not one of us has the right to take another's life even if it is still in the mother's womb. The moment sperm and egg come together—**conception**—is the moment life begins. And at that moment there is **life** with all the sanctity and rights of any life!

A woman does not a possess some sole/sacred right to choose to abort her baby. The man was an equal partner in the sexual act that created life. Where is his "right to choose"? Or where is the baby's right to choose? That baby is a distinct life. Yes, the baby may still be in the mother's womb and certainly is dependent on the mother. And guess what, that baby will be dependent on the mother long after he or she is born. Does the mother still have a "right to abort" her baby say six months after birth? Of course not. How about the father? No. We are missing the reality of life in the abortion discussion. We are missing the *reality of life* in the whole of the LGBTQP movement. This is to say, we have lost our way because we have lost our very souls.

The Divine Touch: A New Creation For Life © 2021

If you do not position the life process (Man and Woman Balance) as the metaphysical primary of life, you will never be able to defend life.

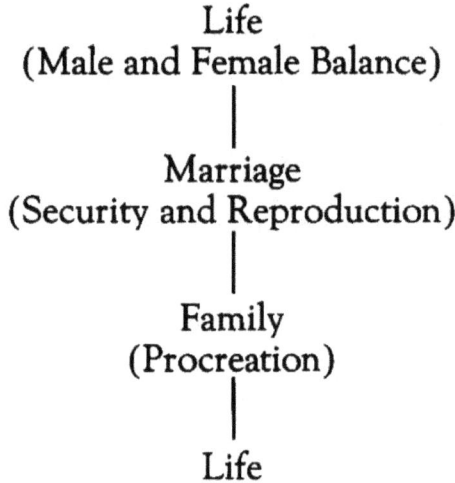

Dimensions in Consciousness © 1990; Selected Writings: Volume 2 © 1991, 2010

Love is not separated from the metaphysic one holds concerning the nature of reality. If that metaphysic is creatively imbalanced, what then does that say about the availability of love? Love springs forth out of creative balance. It is the act of creation itself.

Our Purpose Together—Bringing the Eternal Down to Earth—The 2008-2009 Articles © 2010

Neither masculinism nor feminism, in any of its forms, can bring the eternal down to earth. This is now for us (man and woman pairs) to do. It is our purpose to touch in love together and, by doing so, we, man and woman, bring the eternal down to earth. We do this by living our love in our lives. The eternal is always a procreant balance between metaphysical primaries or duals. There isn't anything more sacred, in the light, or of eternal life than that one procreant touch between one man and one woman right now. That one touch will last forever when you know it.

Our Love is Eternal Love—The 2008-2009 Articles © 2010

Spiritual procreation is the idea/understanding that will lead us to the eternal connection. This universe of ours is one of perfect sexual balance, sexual being equated as equal and opposite. The two forces of (pro)creation perfectly unite and divide over and over. The eternal is no more than the procreant process/lineage. It never began and will never end. It always is what it is and can only be what it is. We may try and circumvent its nature, but that will only be at our own peril.

If we can return to the drawing on Sexual Metaphysics, we can see how we are aborting life. The Man and Woman Relationship holds to life on all three levels, physical, mental, and spiritual. Christianity (or most any religion) aborts life on the spiritual level. Socialism (or any top-down government) aborts life on the spiritual and mental levels. Homosexuality (or LGBTQ) aborts life on the physical, mental, and spiritual levels.

Sexual Metaphysics

Man and Woman Relationship	Christianity	Socialism	Homosexuality
M — S — F	S	S	S
|	|	|	|
M — M — F	M — M — F	M	M
|	|	|	|
M — B — F	M — B — F	M — B — F	B

S—Spirit   M—Mind   B—Body   M—Male   F—Female

Fundamentally, we are not able to leave the creative process of life itself: birth-life-death-rebirth... But we are able to balance each moment in life. Each and every moment awaits our call, *"Come into my heart and receive me into yours."* Now, not tomorrow, but now. *"This one moment of man and woman balance begins...now.*

Perhaps we can begin to correct things by re-establishing Marriage to be between one man and one woman as that is the UNION that begets LIFE?

WWW.MANANDWOMANBALANCE.COM

Walt Whitman (1819-1892)—*Leaves of Grass*, 1855
"This is the nucleus...after the child is born of woman, This is the bath of birth...this is the merge of small and large and the outlet again."

The Touch of Life

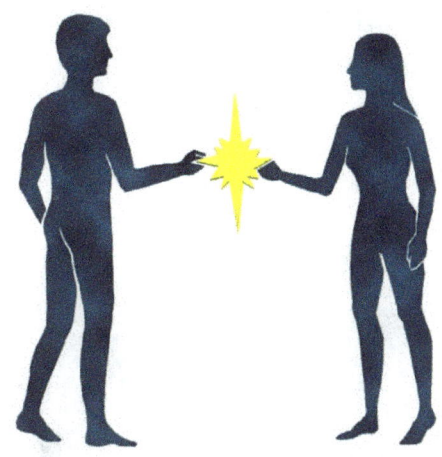

**Our purpose: To bring the message
of Man and Woman Balance to planet Earth!**

But the choice is not easy, is it? *"I have chosen everything but you!"*

Whittaker Chambers (1901-1961)—*Witness*, 1952
"At that end, all men simply pray, and prayer takes as many forms as there are men. Without exception we pray. We pray because there is nothing else to do, and because that is where God is—where there is nothing else."

And not even "God," as we have heretofore defined "Him," will do. Where is the Mother God (equal and opposite) to the Father God? So let it be said one more time, sex (the sexual act) can never be separate from the procreation of life. The spirit of the sexual act is tied into life. When the two sexes come together in union there is a procreation of life. This may not always happen on the physical level but it certainly is happening on the mental level. "I love you," the man says. "And I love you, too," the woman replies. And two hearts become as one. This is the point of **spiritual procreation**. There is nothing more sacred than the two hearts becoming as one. Only a man and a woman (equal and opposite) can unite to again divide.... Even what we call "God" must be sexed:

**If there be a "God the Father" there must also be a
"God the Mother," not a "God the Mother" as a secondary existence to "God the Father," but and an
equal and opposite primary existence to "God the Father."**

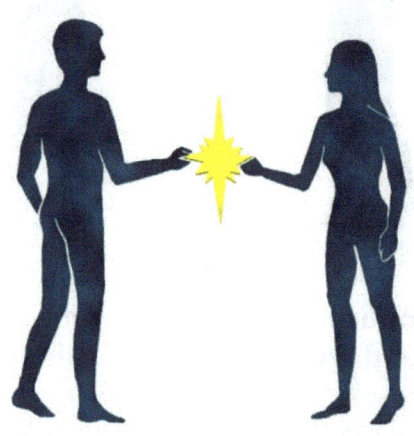

Until we make this spiritual distinction, we are but stuck in nothingness forever.

William Butler Yeats (1865-1939) Irish Poet—*The Second Coming*, 1921

> Things fall apart; the centre cannot hold;
> Mere anarchy is loosed upon the world,
> The blood-dimmed tide is loosed, and everywhere
> The ceremony of innocence is drowned;
> The best lack all conviction, while the worst
> Are full of passionate intensity.

And the thing is, *there aren't any intermediaries.* There is only man and woman—the ***Two Forces of Creation***—touching and creating life together. Man and woman constitute a direct touch. There is no other LIVING TOUCH! Yet we continue to turn to, and hold on to, the religious, political, and sexual imbalances that have ruled our lives since day one. Who is there to speak out?

Fyodor Dostoyevsky (1821-1881), Russian writer
"Nothing is this world is harder than speaking the truth, nothing easier that flattery."

We might add that nothing is more difficult than speaking the truth. You end up being slammed up against yourself.

Ayn Rand (1905-1982)—Writing in her journal at age twenty-three.
"From now on—no thought whatever about yourself, only about your work. You are only a writing engine. Don't stop, until you really and honestly know that you cannot go on."

I have used a number of quotes from Whittaker Chambers' book *Witness*. Why? Because he spoke out. His issue was political. He spoke out against the hidden Communist onslaught that was occurring in his time. Sadly, it is still occurring! And he spoke out until he had no more within himself to speak.

Whittaker Chambers (1901-1961)—*Witness*, 1952
"I am a man who, reluctantly, grudgingly step by step, is destroying himself that this country and the faith by which it lives may continue to exist."

I am speaking out as well, against LGBTQ—no, let me rephrase that. I am not speaking against; I am speaking for:

And if you want a further statement, let us return to a previous quote.

Our Love is Eternal Love—The 2008-2009 Articles © 2010

Spiritual procreation is the idea/understanding that will lead us to the eternal connection. This universe of ours is one of perfect sexual balance, sexual being equated as equal and opposite. The two forces of (pro)creation perfectly unite and divide over and over. The eternal is no more than the procreant process/lineage. It never began and will never end. It always is what it is and can only be what it is. We may try and circumvent its nature, but that will only be at our own peril.

Part 5: The Still Light

What is the still light?

Henry David Thoreau (1817-1862)
"With all your science, can you tell me how it is that light comes into the soul?"

Does anyone know?

Walter Russell (1871-1963)—*The Universal One,* 1926
"Light, as man knows the light is but an unstable simulation of the real light of the Universal One. Man's concept of light is luminosity, an illusion of the universal light of inertia, sustained in its appearance as an illusion of light by the pressures generated through motion. The inner mind of ecstatic man knows the real light and that he is one with the light. He is not deceived by its illusion."

1 John 1: 5: God is light; in him there is no darkness.

Might the Still Light, i.e., God be the name for a living procreative/eternal process? This is the two-force distinction!

Alan Watts (1915-1973)—*Tao: The Watercourse Way,* 1975
"The *yin-yang* principle is not, therefore, what we would ordinarily call a dualism, but rather an explicit duality expressing an implicit unity."

Walter Russell (1871-1963)—*The Divine Iliad,* 1948
"For again I say My one principle of My one law is founded upon the solid rock of equal interchange between all pairs of opposite things, opposite conditions, or opposite transactions between men."

Walt Whitman (1819-1892)—*Leaves of Grass*, 1855

"...Urge and urge and urge, Always the procreant urge of the world. Out of the dimness opposite equals advance..."

Neville Goddard (1905-1972)—*The Power of Awareness*, 1952

"The 'light' is consciousness. Consciousness is *one*, manifesting in legions of forms of levels of consciousness. There is no one that is not *all* that is, for consciousness, though expressed in an infinity series of levels, is not divisional."

Notice how in these quotes there is some confusion regarding Dualism and Unity. Is the Still Light the Unity? But isn't the division of the One into the individual forms of the Two also an essential part of what we call Life. Neville Goddard states, *"Consciousness is one....There is no one that is not all that is, for consciousness, though expressed in an infinity series of levels, is not divisional."* Yet Alan Watts speaks of a *"yin-yang principle is not, therefore, what we would ordinarily call a dualism, but rather an explicit duality expressing an implicit unity."* Walter Russell speaks of *"My one principle of My one law is founded upon the solid rock of equal interchange between all pairs of opposite things, opposite conditions, or opposite transactions between men."* And let's not forget Walt Whitman, *"...Urge and urge and urge, Always the procreant urge of the world. Out of the dimness opposite equals advance..."*

Neville Goddard (1905-1972)—*Awakened Imagination*, 1954

"Duality is an inherent condition of life. Everything that exists is double. Man is a dual creature with contrary principles embedded in his nature. They war within him and present attitudes to life which are antagonistic. This conflict is the eternal enterprise, the war in heaven, the never-ending struggle of the younger or inner man of imagination to assert His supremacy over the elder or outer man of sense."

In this quote Neville Goddard seems to be saying *"Duality is an inherent condition of life."* If duality, the Two, is an inherent condition of life than how can one claim *"Consciousness is one...."*? Again, from Walt Whitman, *Always the procreant urge of the world. Out of the dimness opposite equals advance..."* Is the One a consciousness or a procreant urge? Does a *procreant urge* lie in back of consciousness or at least give to consciousness its impetus into division/form (the Two)? Let's look at one more quote from Neville Goddard.

Neville Goddard (1905-1972)—*Feeling Is The Secret*, 1996

"The subconscious is the womb of creation. It receives the idea unto itself through the feelings of man. It never changes the idea received, but always gives it form. Hence the subconscious out-pictures the idea in the image and likeness of the feeling received. To feel a state as hopeless or impossible is to impress the subconscious with the idea of failure."

In this quote, Neville Goddard is suggesting *"The subconscious is the womb of creation."* Might the subconscious be the one still light, the source/unity point of all differentiated things? *"It never changes the idea received, but always gives it form."* Now, if you are with me, I am suggesting something like Alan Watts: *"The yin-yang principle is not, therefore, what we would ordinarily call a dualism, but rather an explicit duality expressing an implicit unity,"* and Walter Russell: *"For again I say My one principle of My one law is founded upon the solid rock of equal interchange between all pairs of opposite things, opposite conditions, or opposite transactions between men."* We cannot speak of a Oneness of things without at the same time acknowledging the separation or Twoness of things. And vice-versa! Both the Oneness/Unity and Twoness/Duality are in play at all times. And furthermore, the impetus of this Two-way or Two-force process of life is nothing other than *"...Urge and urge and urge, Always the procreant urge of the world."* With this in mind let us ask once more, what is the still light, or as I also refer to it—*the Light behind the Light?*

Webster's New World Dictionary: *1.a) the form of electromagnetic radiation that acts upon the retina of the eye, optic nerve, etc., making sight possible: this energy is transmitted at a velocity of about 186,000 miles per second. 10. Mental illumination; knowledge or information; enlightenment. 11. spiritual inspiration.*

American Dictionary Of The English Language (Webster's 1828 Edition): *1. That ethereal agent or matter which makes objects perceptible to the sense of seeing, but the particles of which are separately invisible. 4. Life. O, springing to light, auspicious babe, be born! Pope. 7. Illuminations of mind; instruction; knowledge. Light, understanding and wisdom was found in him. Dan.v.15. In Scripture, God, the source of knowledge. God is light. 1 John i.16. Christ. That was the true light, that lighteth every man that cometh into the world. John i.*

Dictionary of Philosophy and Religion: *The analysis of light through much of the history of philosophy has been at the same time physical and divine illumination. The Neoplatonic doctrine treated light in dual terms. It was an emanation of the divine, containing both physical and spiritual aspects. Out of the Neoplatonic tradition, however, other analyses emerged. (1) Robert Grosseteste held light to be the 1st principle of material things, which transformed itself into other elements. (2) Witelo accepted the Neoplatonic analysis but also studied the phenomenon of light directly through optics. (3) Descartes and Newton held to a corpuscular theory of light, treating it as a physical phenomenon. (4) Einstein demonstrated that the velocity of light is constant, and that its rays would bend when passing through a strong gravitational field.*

The Donning International Encyclopedic Psychic Dictionary: *1. An unorganized, luminous, radiant, electromagnetic energy presenting itself in the beginning; a* *primeval source of* TOTAL INTELLIGENCE; *indestructible in its original state, but capable of breaking up into manifestations of other shapes, textures, and sizes with varying degrees of this intelligence. 2. Essence of all* MATTER; *a wave motion of particles within the* ETHER *which is within matter; now manifests in all the universe in an orderly intelligent manner.*

Walt Whitman (1819-1892)—*Leaves of Grass*, 1855
Song for Myself
"I have heard what the talkers were talking....the talk of the beginning and the end,
But I do not talk of the beginning or the end.
There was never any more inception than there is now,
Nor any more youth or age than there is now;
And will never be any more perfection than there is now,
Nor any more heaven or hell than there is now.
Urge and urge and urge,
Always the procreant urge of the world.
Out of the dimness opposite equals advance...Always substance and increase.
Always a knit of identity....always distinction....always a breed of life."

I Sing the Body Electric
"This is the nucleus...after the child is born of woman,
This is the bath of birth...this is the merge of small and large and the outlet again."

My suggestion is that the Still Light is a name (like God) for the whole of the **Sexual Procreant Process of Male and Female Division and Unification**. We can also use the terms Unity, Oneness, or even Ether. But there also is, and must be, the point of Division, equal to but opposite from the point of Unity. In other words, both come together. Unity is not prior to Division. Division is not superior to Unity. Man is not superior to Woman. Woman is not ever without Man. Both come together. Both constitute the Still

Light, not individually but collectively. In fact, there is neither a singular individually nor a singular unity. Both <u>together</u> constitute the whole of a **Procreant Process of Life**—or what can be called Birth-Life-Death-Rebirth. And so the Ether is but an **Eternal Procreant Process of Life**.

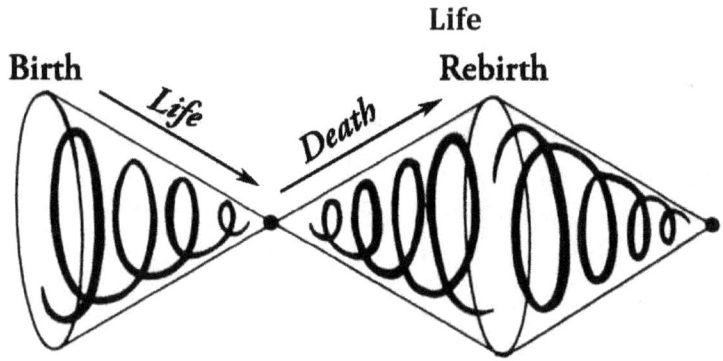

Wealth Plus⁺ Empowering Your Everyday! © 2014
Connecting your light with the light behind the world.

Your light shines with the individual moment-by-moment decision to give more to and take less from another. When you and another meet together in this <u>connection</u>, a light shines from behind the world. It is this connection that gives light to the world. Your connection together, in whatever its form, gives light to culture and values. Culture and values only live in light. All light, as mentioned, *is both static and dynamic in its nature. Light propagates (reproduces) itself through its two equal yet opposing forces. It can be said that light is a static/dynamic balance between two equal yet opposing forces.* Your every thought/action is balanced—in its connection with another. Your every thought/action is wealth producing—in its connection with another. Balance and connection are one. Connection and love are one. Love and wealth are one. Within the connection is the perfect separation/expression of balance, wealth, and love. Within the separation is the connection. *One is not without the other; both are needed for either to be.* Know light as your love with your equal and opposite sexual other half right now.

Wealth is (spiritually) contained in a statement.

A statement for your wealth attainment will now be given to you. The statement is not to be explained. You will know in your heart and soul its meaning although you may not understand its correlation to wealth creation/attraction. Just trust the statement. If it does not fit with your current beliefs just acknowledge that. The statement cannot in anyway harm you. It holds to your deepest needs and concerns. Say it over and over until it is memorized into your being. Let it do its work inside of you. It will clean out all the old negative/poverty thought patterns within you leaving only wealth in your life now.

"God" is light. Light attracts light. Light is both static and dynamic in its nature. Light propagates (reproduces) itself through its two equal yet opposing forces. It can be said that light is a static/dynamic balance between two equal yet opposing forces. The forces are known as male and female. Male and female are the two forces of the universe. They are equal and opposite, i.e., sexual, in nature at all times. They comprise the united one (the static) which then becomes the divided two (the dynamic)... a procreant life process/lineage. Male is the force of their division; female the force of their union. "God" (or use the terms order, light, or balance) then is an unseen yet universal, automatic yet intentive, living two-way (dividing and uniting) sexual process--connecting the souls of a man and a woman to each other (from the very beginning) with a specific purpose, fundamental and necessary for the wealth attainment of all mankind. <u>This specific purpose/connection is the center point of wealth itself.</u> Be it. Know it. Embrace your equal and opposite procreant other half who is spiritually with you now and at all times. Feel that glow. It is your light together. The universe is alive with your light together. This sharing of your (equal and opposite) lights, on whatever level, with each other is known as love. Together, your only natures are love. Together, your only functions are to express to each other your love. Love is wealth. Love always

exists to be expressed, one to another. Such is the purpose and point of action--expressing love...one to another. Within your love together is all the wealth that can ever exist.

Now take a moment—notice that a burden has just been lifted from your shoulders. Your stress and despair are fading from you. That negativity of "I can't" is being replaced by the certainty of "I can and will." In the following days, notice how new ideas, opportunities, and abilities are coming to you. Something you have been waiting for (and have almost given up on) is on its way to you as well. And for the first time you feel empowered and know that this time that feeling is not going to go away. Life appears beautiful, natural, and without effort because it is. Wealth Plus⁺ now exists in your soul!

THE
DIVINE TOUCH

A NEW CREATION FOR LIFE

"I see a light no man or woman has ever seen. The unseen world is now the seen and known world; its order is beautiful, its balance perfect. Yes, I see a new world, the most Divine world that has ever come to pass. And I can even <u>prove</u> it to you, for, you see, I now see You."

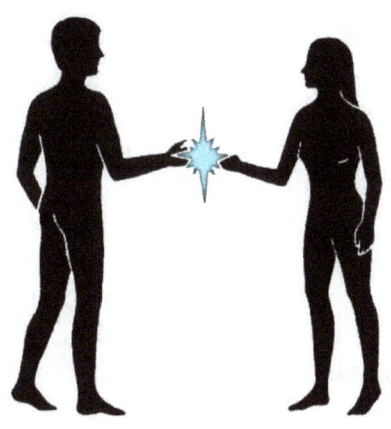

The Divine Touch: A New Creation for Life © 2021

Part 6: Etheric Materialization Into Form

I have spoken of the Light behind the Light. What this refers to is the **Spiritual Light** behind the physical light. It even means the Spiritual Light behind the mental faculty/clarity. The Light behind the (physical or mental) light is also known as the Still Light. It actually is the Unity Point in the Male and Female Procreant Process of Birth-Life-Death-Rebirth. Let's remember that Death is but the resting point, a point of Unity in the (Equal and Opposite) Procreant Process of Life.

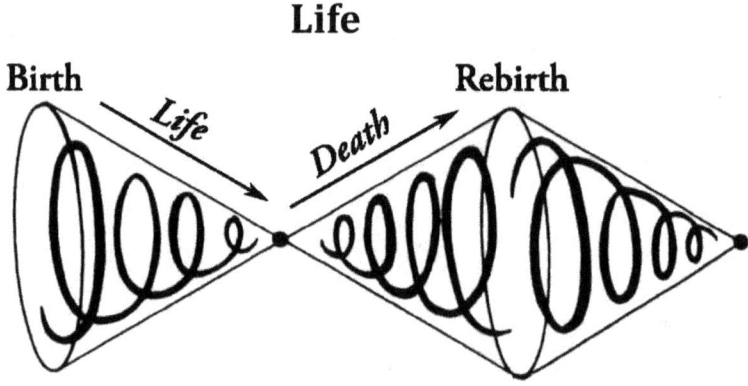

The key, and missing link, to the Procreant Process of Life is that it is <u>Procreative</u>. Mankind has missed the necessity of this Procreant element. ***The frame and nature of life is procreative!*** The Universe is procreant in its nature. The Universe is a living, breathing, two force birth-life-death-rebirth eternal process. As such we may give it the name—***The Eternal Given!***

The Light at the End of the Mind: Meditations for Deepening Love © 1994; Expanded Edition © 2010

It simply is what it is and cannot be what it is not.

The light at the end of the mind illuminates the mind with all clarity. Clarity—a purity of constant realization that this light could only reside at the end of the mind. After all ideas have come into awareness—without an answer. After all action from these ideas have been taken—to no avail. After all hope has been lost, and finally admitted to, here comes the last idea. Yes, the light at the end of the mind is but an *idea*. An idea that is a *word*--a word that contains all the meaning of life and illuminates the mind with the understanding that has been missing since the dawn of consciousness. The light at the end of the mind is the last idea to be brought to consciousness. It is the final idea of all mankind. It is the one idea all have been waiting for. It is the one idea that will organize all disorder out of the mind. It is the one idea that will free the spirit of all envy. It is the one idea that will relieve the heart of all burden. But this idea will only do that if it is put in its proper perspective as the single and center point of all existence. There is to be no greater idea. There is to be no more significant understanding. There is to be no more enduring truth. Not that we or anyone is to bow down to this idea. It stands only as the central organizing factor of all thought and action, bringing clarity to our lives and everything we do or aspire to. The light at the end of the mind, that exists as an idea and is known through a word, is now ready to illuminate a mind.

The light at the end of the mind is not necessarily a new idea. It has been heard before. But never has it been uttered in its proper context. Never has it been known as the final idea, as the greatest idea, as an idea that encompasses the whole of the understanding, bringing all order to that understanding. The idea, cherished by few, has conveniently been relegated to second tier by mankind in his/her religious, political, and sexual belief systems. The great religious and philosophical books presenting the great ideas of mankind forget to mention it. Your author remembers seeing it only one time.* You, the reader, when you hear this idea, may think you already know about it, that you have superior knowledge and are not moved. But let me impress upon you, this idea has yet to be understood in its *spiritual* significance. I assure you, you will not know what that significance is. You must allow the idea into your mind free of your own preconceptions and let it do its work. *Let it work in you.* If left to do its work, it will reorganize your mind and free your heart such that a light will begin to grow, and glow, within you—the light at the end of the mind.

Leaves of Grass—Walt Whitman, 1855

The idea that is a word that exists as the light at the end of the mind only exists at the end of the mind. If this idea does not crush you with its simplicity, if it does not freeze you with its purity, if it does not release you in it universality, if it does not center you in its totality, if it does not extend you in its density, if it does not embrace you with its clarity, please do not enter its gates. I know you want to read on and see what this *word* is but don't, for this word only exists at the end of the mind. You can only see it from that vantage point. If you haven't yet *lost your own mind,* don't read on. If you haven't yet had *your spirit crushed,* don't read on. If you haven't yet *lost all faith* in the immensity of faith, don't read on. If you haven't yet discovered it was never about you or not about you, don't read on. If you are not ready for instant enlightenment, don't read on—the light at the end of the mind is the brightest of lights. It has already blinded all those who cannot see.

The light at the end of the mind is but an idea that is a word. It does not need an explanation. In fact, it cannot be explained. It is what is called *self-evident.* Its meaning will be instantly known. The light at the end of the mind has always been known. Admitted to or not, agreed to or not, it will be recognized as truth. To those of you who have questions, none will be answered. To those of you who have doubts—they are your own. To those of you who speak ill of this word, you will feel a darkness surround you. This is not personal nor is this stated as some absolute judgment. You see, there isn't any subjective compromise to be had. We just are not able to place our subjective desires into the metaphysical structure and constraints of the universe. Subjective compromise has always been our downfall. The light at the end of the mind cannot compromise. *It simply is what it is and cannot be what it is not.* The light at the end of the mind is always and only what it is. It has always been what it is and has never been what it is not. It will always be what it is and will never be what it is not. The light at the end of the mind is, and can only be, an idea that is a word. That word is ***procreant***.

There is another name we can give to this Procreant Process of Life, i.e., the Eternal Given, and that is the Etheric. I touched on this in the last part. Let's continue. According the Wikipedia: *"The etheric body, ether-body, or aether body is a subtle body propounded in esoteric and occult philosophies as the first or lowest layer in the human energy field or aura. The etheric body is said to be in immediate contact with the physical body and to sustain it and connect it with 'higher' bodies."* Dictionary. Com states: 1.: *"of or relating to the heavens: heavenly. 2.: being light and airy: delicate, ethereally."*

Let's look at the term Ether. This is from Oxford Languages Dictionary: *"Referred to as 'akasha' in Sanskrit, ether is the element that comes first in yogic and ayurvedic thinking. Ether is without the firmness of earth, the coolness of water, the heat of fire or even the movement of wind. It is therefor the very essence of 'emptiness'. The space element is the most subtle of all elements."* Again from Wikipedia: *"ether, in physics, a theoretical universal substance believed during the 19th century to act as the medium for transmission of electromagnetic waves (e.g., light and X-rays), much as sound waves are transmitted by elastic media such as air."*

As I understand it the existence of the ether cannot be proved/verified. Perhaps ether corresponds to the Unity as I refer to it. Unity is that state where no differentiation/substance exists. It is the opposite of Division/Individuality. We may call it Oneness in contract to Twoness. As I am presenting things, there are two metaphysical forces; the One must divide and the Two must unite. Again, let's look at the example of breathing—Inhalation divides, Exhalation unites. ***One is not without the other; both are needed for either to be!*** Such as in Life: Birth (or effort) is the division, death (or rest) is the unification. Furthermore, male is the desire/force to divide the One and female is the desire/force to unite the Two.

The Eternal Process of Male and Female Division and Unification

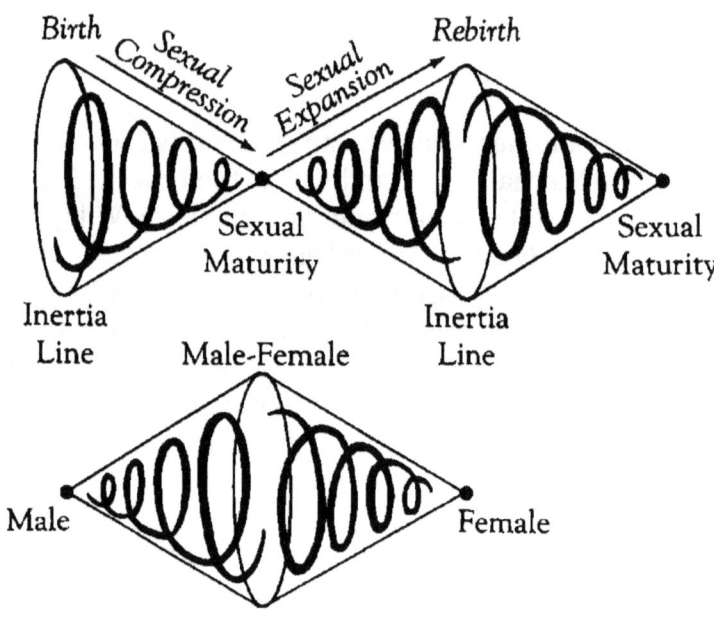

A problem arises when we attempt to verify the Unification of all things. With division, separate things stand right before our eyes. But how can we "prove" the unification of all things. How can Science measure/prove that which does not have differentiation? (Maybe that is the work of those who meditate—to be in the experience of Oneness.) The Light behind the Light is but the Unification of all things—one part of the two-part process of division and unification. Such is the Ether. And yet from the Ether (may we also call it the WOMB?) all (separate) things are given birth. You see, we LIVE in a Co-Existent Universe—I Am and You

Are! Each one of us is a **Sexual Presence** with the purpose to divide the one (male) or unite the two (female). What we call the Christ is not a specific person perse; but a state of mind/heart. We might say the Christ state is co-presence or co-existence. We can't get to the Christ state without an understanding of the balance between the sexual two. In the balance there is LOVE. **John 13:14:** *A new commandment I give unto you, That ye love one another; as I have loved you, that ye also love one another.* Unfortunately, we are not able to do this. We have yet to incorporate the SEXUAL BALANCE OF LIFE on the three planes of Life—Spiritual, Mental, and Physical. Our religions come close; so does New Thought, and specifically A Course in Miracles. I don't mean to slam these other avenues but we just cannot get to the Still Light, i.e., Etheric (Sexual) Frame within ourselves and touch another for we have yet to balance each other within our hearts and souls. You might say we have yet to make clean our own Hearts/Souls. So how can we materialize what we want if we are not clean? We can't.

Dimensions in Consciousness: © 1990; Selected Writings: Volume 2: © 1991, 2010
Love is not separated from the metaphysic one holds concerning the nature of reality. If that metaphysic is creatively imbalanced, what then does that say about the availability of love? Love springs forth out of creative balance. It is the act of creation itself.

Many a great thinker has pointed to a way, a path forward.
Jesus of Nazareth – Blessed are the pure in heart: for they shall see God.
Thomas Troward – Originating Creative Principle of Life.
Neville Goddard – Law of Inverse Transformation.
Walter Russell – Thou, my Father-Mother, are the Light of the world.
Meister Eckhart – In the eternal birth, the soul becomes pure and one.
Leo Tolstoy – All, everything that I understand, I understand only because I love.
Christopher Anderson – One is not without the other; both are needed for either to be.

Yes, I have included myself. Perhaps not so great. That's not the point. So what is missing? Maybe it is faith and prayer and forgiveness?

Robert A. Russell (1947-2023)—*God Works Through Faith*

"Prayer is the realization of our Oneness with God and the acceptance of the tremendous power this realization gives us."

Neville Goddard (1905-1972)—*Prayer - The Art of Believing*, 1945

"A feeling is always accompanied by a corresponding vibration, that is, a change in expression or sensation in the operator.

There is no thought or feeling without expression...."

Kahlil Gibran (1883-1931)—*The Prophet*, 1923

"Prayer is but the expansion of yourself into the living ether. When you pray, you rise to meet in the air those who are praying at that very hour, and whom save in prayer you may not meet. Therefore let your visit to the temple invisible be for naught save ecstasy and sweet communion. I cannot teach you to pray in words. God listens not to your words save when He 'Him'self utters them through your lips."

Prayer turns into **answered prayer** when it touches the helm of Grace. And what is Grace but a state of love, one to another? And in that love there is perfect balance: I Am and You Are!

Florence Sovel Shinn (1871-1940)—*The Game of Life and How to Play It*, 1925

"Only that which is true of God is true of me, for I and the Father are ONE.

"As I am one with God, I am one with my good, for God is both the *Giver* and the *Gift*. I cannot separate the *Giver* from the *Gift*.

"Every plan my Father in heaven has not planned, shall be dissolved and dissipated, and the Divine Idea now comes to pass.

"Divine love now dissolves and dissipates every wrong condition in my mind, body, and affairs. Divine love is the most powerful chemical in the universe, and *dissolves everything* which is not of itself!

"Divine Love floods my consciousness with health, and every cell in my body is filled with light.

"My eyes are God's eyes, I see with the eyes of spirit. I see clearly the open way; there are no obstacles on my pathway. I see clearly the perfect plan.

"I call on the law of forgiveness. I am free from mistakes and the consequences of mistakes. I am under grace and not under karmic law. I forgive everyone and everyone forgives me. The gates swing open for my good.

"I cast this burden on the Christ within, and I go free!"

Neville Goddard (1905-1972)—*Resurrection*

"The subconscious is the womb of creation. It receives the idea unto itself through the feelings of man. <u>It never changes the idea received, but always gives it form</u>. Hence the subconscious out-pictures the idea in the image and likeness of the feeling received. To feel a state as hopeless or impossible is to impress the subconscious with the idea of failure."

Agostino Degas

"Nothing happens in the universe. Everything is connected from invisible to invisible wires. When the right time comes, extraordinary meetings among people who have been waiting forever, happen with the same simplicity and naturalness with which a flower blooms."

Christian D. Larson (1874-1954)—*The Ideal Made Real*

"The prayer that is uttered through the spirit of faith and through the soul of thanksgiving—the two united in one, is always answered, whether it be uttered silently or audibly."

Max Freedom Long (1890-1971)—*What Jesus Taught in Secret*, 1983

"It is the Father-Mother who is appealed to in prayer and on whose 'name' we must call."

And yet, so many of us have climbed the tall mountain only to find—what? **Nothingness**. I am reminded of the song, "A Long and Winding Road" by the Beatles. (Also sung by George Michael.) Cuts into the heart. In all roads offered and taken we find <u>Nothing</u>. Look at our religions, our politics, and LGBTQ—**Nothing.**

George Orwell (1903-1950)—*1984*

"The most terrible loneliness is not the kind that comes from being alone, but the kind that comes from being misunderstood. It is the loneliness of standing in a crowded room, surrounded by people who do not see you, who do not hear you, who do not know the true essence of who you are. And in that loneliness, you feel as though you are fading, disappearing into the background, until you are nothing more than a ghost, a shadow of your former self."

Let's return to the quote by Emanuel Swedenborg.

Emanuel Swedenborg (1688-1772)—*The Sensible Joy in Married Love and The Foolish Pleasures of Illicit Love*, 1768

"The principle of marriage is like the balance in which that love is weighed. For the marriage principle of one man with one wife is the precious treasure of human life and the treasure of the Christian religion.... So married love is attributed to someone after death according to the rational life of his spirit. And one whom that love is implanted in is provided a marriage in heaven after death, whatever kind of marriage he had in the world."

That quote is a mouth full. Can our religions, politics, or LGBTQ take that on? *"And one whom that love is implanted in is provided a marriage in heaven after death, whatever kind of marriage he had in the world."* So close it is, yet something is still missing. You see, we have not understood something so important that until we do we can't move forward. You see, **The soul of a woman has been hurt!** And so, every child is born in what we call "original sin." It is not really the sin of woman; it is the sin of man. Man, that is men, have used women since day one to satisfy his (sexual) desires. There is a beauty in the union of man and woman. But for man to use his physical, and even mental, power to sexually use a woman for his own need yet not touch her in love and commitment is the sin. And that sin is passed down to the children.

The Soul Of A Woman Has Been Hurt

So, the answer will come but only after we have understood that the soul of a woman has been hurt. In Christian terms we must alter the frame from God the Father, God the Son, and God the Holy Ghost to God the Father, God the Mother, and God the Holy Son or **Holy Daughter**. We must bring forth woman as an equal necessity to man. This constitutes a metaphysical shift to the understanding of a two sexual forces, equal in necessity yet opposite in function.

This shift can only come about when we understand and feel within ourselves:

Can this be done or does the heart of man insist he is King? Do not men continue to view woman as secondary?

Man, Woman, and God © 1994, 2010
Men, do you know that the soul of woman has been hurt? You have hurt your woman, haven't you? You left her behind to bleed on the roadside. You used and discarded her when all she wanted was to love you. Why do you do this? Do you not see that woman is the only bridge that will take you beyond yourself? Woman is your only hope, but due to your actions she is giving up her belief in you. Can you, man, take responsibility for creating this state of affairs? Can you feel every pain that you have ever caused woman, from her birth to her death?

And how do women often react? In their hurt, at least today, they offer us feminism/Diversity, Equity, and Inclusion.

Man, Woman, and God © 1994, 2010

Women, do you know the spirit of man has been hurt? You blame man for all the havoc around you, don't you? You think that men "just don't get it" and that you could do a better job at life. Can you? In the name of equality, you kill the spirit of life, the difference that you and men depend upon. Now, you only want a man conditionally, not completely. Cannot you see that without a man you can't even have yourself? Perhaps men, too, are doing the best they know how and that in their hearts they only want to care for you. Will you allow that? Can you feel a man's very struggle throughout all of time to do only one thing, to make a home for you? Can you feel this when you are alone?

The woman is reacting to her own hurt. Her nature is love. The man, in wanting his sex without commitment, brings a hurt to the woman that has yet to be healed. Are there good men and women out there? Yes. Think of all the mothers and fathers who do their best for their children. Think of all the young men who have been mowed down in another endless war. Of what benefit are these wars? Perhaps to cover-up the counterfeit money cabal not to mention the trafficking of drugs, women, and children.

To All Men the World Over

To those of you who claim to know God, or some kind of human goodness...

Be it now known:

- As you treat a woman, so do you treat God.
- As you honor a woman, so do you honor God.
- As you love a woman, so do you love God.
- As you hold tight to a woman, so do you hold tight to God.
- As you listen to a woman, so do you hear God.
- As you respect a woman, so do you respect God.

- As you stand up for a woman, so do you stand up for God.
- As you walk with a woman, so do you walk with God.
- As you trust in a woman, so do you trust in God.
- As you cherish a woman, so do you cherish God.
- As you believe in a woman, so do you believe in God.
- As you have a child with a woman, so you have a child of God.
- As you hold to the very center of creation with a woman, so do you hold to the very center of creation with God.
- As you no longer look for God other than in a woman, so do you know the love of God.

Let it now be known—your only avenue to God is in touching the very heart of a woman.

Wealth Plus+: Empowering Your Everyday! © 2014

The Prime Movers: The Sovereigncy of Man and Woman © 2015

You align to Source by giving your love to your sexual other half. A man gives his (securitive) love to a woman; a woman gives her (reproductive) love to a man. *That is all there is.* We don't need to concern ourselves about "loving ourselves," as if one could. Our only concern is to love our sexual other half. Do you hear this? *Only the action of giving your love to your sexual other half will keep you in alignment to Source such that the Law of Attraction will work for you.* Why is this so? Because you are one (of the two) sexual Prime Mover<u>s</u>.

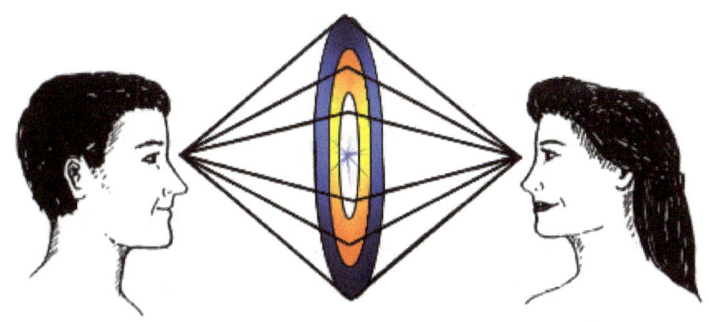

Let us understand, the Unity, the Oneness, The Still Light, the Etheric Universal Substance is but the Soul/Womb of Woman. Woman is space, man is matter. Without periodic union with Woman, Man cannot progress. Man cannot have Life. A man's seed/soul must be implanted into womb/woman for there to be a **Birth of Life**. And at that exact moment where the two become as one a new life begins—either as male or as female. "And where there was one there is now a (sexual) two."

William Wordsworth (1770-1850) English Poet—*She Was A Phantom of Delight*

> She was a Phantom of delight
> When first she gleamed upon my sight;
> A lovely Apparition, sent
> To be a moment's ornament;
> Her eyes as stars of Twilight fair;
> Like Twilight's, too, her dusky hair;
> But all things else about her drawn
> From May-time and the cheerful Dawn;
> A dancing Shape, an Image gay,
> To haunt, to startle, and way-lay.
> I saw her upon nearer view,
> A Spirit, yet a Woman too!
> Her household motions light and free,
> And steps of virgin-liberty;
> A countenance in which did meet
> Sweet records, promises as sweet;
> A Creature not too bright or good

For human nature's daily food;
For transient sorrows, simple wiles,
Praise, blame, love, kisses, tears, and smiles.
And now I see with eye serene
The very pulse of the machine;
A Being breathing thoughtful breath,
A Traveller between life and death;
The reason firm, the temperate will,
Endurance, foresight, strength, and skill;
A perfect Woman, nobly planned,
To warn, to comfort, and command;
And yet a Spirit still, and bright
With something of angelic light.

To Cassandra—Early Years © 1985 1994

I, Cassandra, Will Come

Do not despair, my love
I, Cassandra, will come
To you very shortly.
I know you have waited patiently
And worked so very hard
To show us the way
Out of the impasse
Of our own cosmic blunder.
Yes, I will come soon.
(Are you calling for me now?)
And when we unite
The world will then know
The way into the light.

The Man and Woman Manifesto: What We Believe! © 2017

So our spiritual task is only to *love ye one another.* In these simple four words all karma is released. Our inner or spiritual cord is reset. Do you see the difference in this balance and what we call worship? We are not here to worship "God" and the like. In fact, that is only an indication that one is not understanding the two-force sexual balance. There isn't anything beyond *love ye one another.* There isn't any Jesus to wait for or some special place/heaven we go to (after life) that is outside of, prior to, or different from *love ye one another.* "There is only a man and a woman, touching and expressing creation together."

And so it is now known that we, You and I, male and female together, comprise the *original light.* All the light in the universe is within us now. All the "God" that exists is within us now. We, You and I, man and woman, are interconnected now. We, man and woman, are procreating all the life and love there is now. And it is from this perfect *sexual* balance, and this perfect *sexual* balance alone, that we want to look at the spiritual task of *creative manifestation* also called **Etheric Materialization Into Form**.

The Divine Touch: A New Creation for Life © 2021

Man and Woman Balance is just a balance. It is not a religion, or even a belief system. It is just a real life <u>sexual</u> balance, and, as such, it is a *direct touch*, man to woman and woman to man. There isn't any other or better world or reality out there. There is only this moment of Man and Woman Balance.

A direct touch, man to woman, woman to man, is not just physical. It is also spiritual. We need to enlarge the understanding of sex to include its spiritual nature. And, in so doing, we will also realize that: ***The Holy Spirit is Woman.*** Man is the force of division; woman is the force of unification. A woman stands between man and child. She connects man and child. She holds life within her DNA. She rests all life within her womb. Men, you cannot do one thing, make one move or build something better, a new invention, without giving it all over to woman. She is the connection point; you are the point of individualization.

> **John 14:16:** And I will pray the Father, and he shall give you another Comforter, that he may abide with you forever.

> **John 14:26:** But the Comforter, which is the Holy Ghost, whom the Father will send in my name, he shall teach you all things, and bring all things to your remembrance, whatsoever I have said unto you.

Yes, the Holy Spirit is Woman. I call her the Eternal Woman. Let's hear her speak.

Channeling the Eternal Woman © 2014

Thank you. I am the *Eternal Woman*. I am not a "God." I am a woman. I am the female soul within every woman. As a woman, I stand with man. Actually, I stand between man and child. I am the link between man and child. I am the space between man and child. I am the death of all life and the life of all death. From a man dying inside of me, so our child is born out of me. I am what you might call the field, frame, zero-point, space, opening, womb, or void. But I am not death. Rather, I give life to death. I bring life-potential to all things. I connect all things within me. In this, I am love. Without me there would never be love. All women know this about me because they know it about themselves.

Men, don't ever disregard a woman, for only <u>together</u> can you continue to secure and reproduce LIFE. There just isn't a point of singularity in the universe. Everything we do begins from a contraction and ends in an expansion. Everything we do we do together. ***One is not without the other; both are needed for either to be.*** This is the balance—the ***Cosmic Mirror*** if you will.

The Prime Mover<u>s</u>
make the sexual abstraction between
(one) order and (two) forces and thereby become
the Prime Mover<u>s</u>!

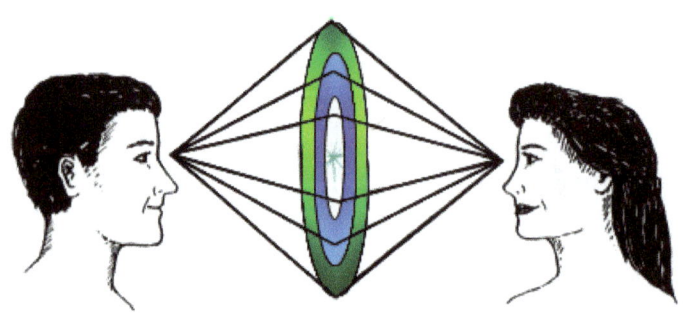

The Prime Movers: The Sovereign<u>c</u>y of Man and Woman © 2015

Channeling the Eternal Woman © 2014

I want you to know that I, the Eternal Woman, answer each and every prayer request made to me. Actually, all prayers are to me. As I have said, I am the space or field. Some call me the eternal void. But I am not empty space or a field without miracles. I am the tomb that all individual things die into and I am the womb that gives rebirth to all individual things. Know me as fertility. I will give rebirth to whatever you give to me. I am *perfect balance*. Each and every prayer that you asketh of me, I replay back to you as to your <u>intent</u>. Did you hear me? I give back to you in equal measure as per your intention. Could I do otherwise?

Now let us set some parameters for **Etheric Materialization Into Form**.

Cassandra speaks:

You who heareth my prayer. Let my words pierce your very soul. It is not enough to just hear my words. You must feel them in your heart which is also your universal soul. Your universal soul is connected to the Etheric Plane. They are one. But within the Etheric Plane is a primary need. Let us use the term REBIRTH. You have come to me for <u>rebirth</u>. Let us reflect on the following:

The Etheric Plane is a living substance. It is one of the two parameter points of what you call Life. The other parameter point is rebirth into individual form.

Co-presence, co-existence, co-creation; I Am and You are.

The Holy Spirit as Ether/Unity/Female.

Forgiveness lies in the recognition that the spirit of Woman is the Holy Spirit.

The magnetic field is female; the gravitational field is male.

Prayer is heart to heart connection. The touch is made!

The subconscious mind (female) reacts immediately to all requests.

The Universal Womb—Man, place your desire-seed into the womb of Woman. Woman, receive the soul-seed into your womb that you may give it reproduction. This may be done spiritually.

Balance is the Cosmic Mirror.

The spiritual word for Balance is Grace.

We enter into the Etheric Space through Grace. Grace equals Truth. Truth equals Balance. Balance equals Love.

Grace is not unmerited. It is absolute balance—the God state itself.

Grace and Faith—Not supernatural. The heart of God is not different from the heart of You or I.

Grace is balance at the Spiritual Level. The balance is between male and female. This must be the essence of our Faith.

The nervous system is like the subconscious mind. It records all feelings.

Prayer is a Touch, a Heart Connection.

Men: Ask from your heart and you shall receive as you give.

Women: Receive into your heart—You are pure spirit—so that you may beget all things.

And in your Touch together there is life. There is love. There is eternal Grace.

Grace is a word much overlooked. It is the spiritual word for balance. Everything is in a balance with it sexual (equal and opposite) other half. Men, what have you done? Did you think you could create alone? There isn't any singular creation. Everything you bring forth reflects how you treat a woman. She is your Holy Spirit. Include her in all you say and do. Give to her your very life. She will reproduce everything you give to her. Remember, you don't just live unto yourself; you live with her and for her as well. And in you two coming together as one, so will your next division/creation, your very child, be born into life.

The same holds true for anything you produce/create. Hold it in the Grace that is you and your sexual other half. In so doing you touch the soul of everyone. We have given the name Art to such spiritual creations. So men, spiritually plant the seed of your desire into the heart/soul of woman. Touch her in SPIRIT. And women, receive that spiritual seed into your being so you may unite with it and give birth to it as the perfect expression of your Touch in Heart—Together as One.

"But when, when will <u>my</u> prayer be answered?"

A prayer is answered only as it is asked for in Grace. Faith is the knowing that you, in your asking, have just touched in Grace.

"When is that?"

Right now. It is in your heart right now. Not just in your mind but your heart. The heart is the connective agent. What lies in one's heart is one's truth. It is also one's TOUCH. And your touch *lives* in you right now. Just ask and you shall receive. Just spiritually give it to another *in grace* and let your desire appear. And then regive it.

Our Love is Eternal Love—The 2008 - 2009 Articles © 2010

Spiritual procreation is the idea/understanding that will lead us to the eternal connection. This universe of ours is one of perfect sexual balance, sexual being equated as equal and opposite. The two forces of (pro)creation perfectly unite and divide over and over. The eternal is no more than the procreant process/lineage. It never began and will never end. It always is what it is and can only be what it is. We may try and circumvent its nature, but that will only be at our own peril.

Let There Be Life! © 2024

The message of Man and Woman Balance is simply about a TOUCH, one unto another. The TOUCH is the BALANCE is the PROCREANT! This spiritual touch transcends time. It also transcends death.... This is the TOUCH. You can call it ETERNAL LIFE. I call it SPIRITUAL PROCREATION. LET THERE BE LIFE!

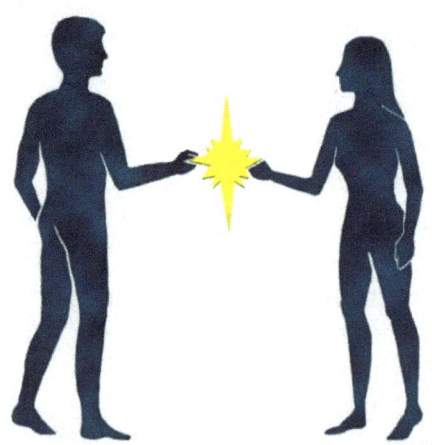

The Miracle of Life*

The miracle of life is that the whole of the universe/life is based on male and female procreant love without which there wouldn't be any universe/life!

*The Prime Movers: The Sovereigncy of Man and Woman, 2015

Selected Writings – Volume 2 © 1991, 2010

My friends, you who are the last and the first man and woman, perfect in your love together. You have prepared a place. Your children await. Go out upon the lands and be fruitful and multiply your love upon this earth.

Eternal Life

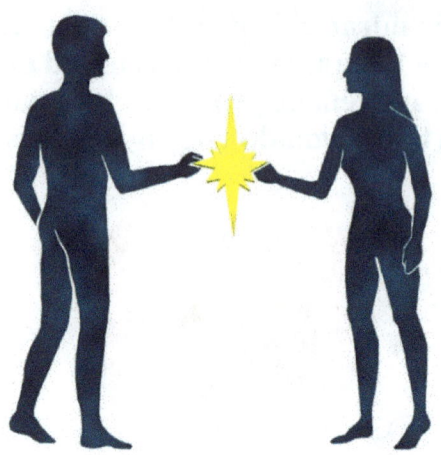

Let's take a moment and balance our souls in the acknowledgement of the **pure love** that exists between ourselves and our equal and opposite sexual other half right now.

John 13:14: A new commandment I give unto you, That ye love one another; as I have loved you, that ye also love one another.

And so, let us begin to pray together. Not necessarily in groups but in the understanding that you can never pray for yourself alone. You are always interconnected. I Am and You Are! Pray in the balance.

Love Ye One Another
Conscious presence (I am and You are)
Balance/Surrender to the Still Light
Joy/Inspiration
Synchronicity
Channeling/Remote viewing
Spiritual Purity/Rebirth
Levitation of the Soul
Materialization into Form

Love ye one another, this is our beginning point. It is also our ending point; actually, our only point. So, take a moment and place your desire into the perfect balance, i.e., the Cosmic Mirror, between you and your sexual other half. This is a spiritual enterprise, i.e., a Source Consciousness. **Etheric Materialization Into Form** is simply the *Universal Sexual Division and Unification Living Process between Man and Woman*. And may you now understand, and feel within yourself, that you are not alone. You are always in an interconnection with your equal and opposite eternal other half. *Giving and Receiving*. Don't ask or pray for yourself alone but for **"I Am and You Are!"** Ask and pray for in OUR name. OUR being you and your eternal other half.

> **Man:** "I plant my desire/seed into your perfect Unity and see it come back to me more than that which I have asked for so I can give to you once more."
>
> **Woman:** "I receive your desire/seed and unite it with my own, creating our perfect Unity from which our next Division shall occur, bringing to us all that we have desired, and even more."

The Prime Movers
discover Source Consciousness and thereby
create a living universe of procreative love!

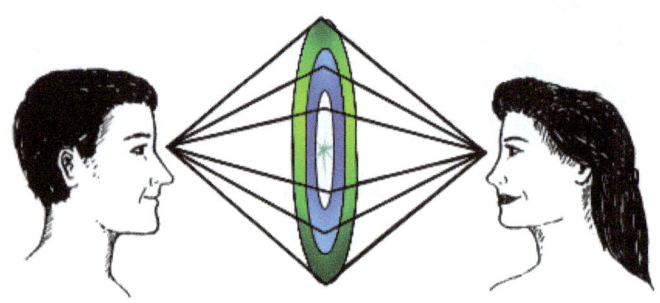

The Prime Movers: The Sovereignty of Man and Woman © 2015

If I man conclude this writing with three passages from *The Life of Jehoshua, The Prophet of Nazareth* by Franz Hartmann. You may recall that I was quite favorable of the earlier passages I quoted from in his writing. In summation he stated: "The real Christ means *Universal Life*, while the 'Christ' of the sects means separateness and favouritism." Yes, I agree. But, I wonder, where is there mention of male and female, i.e., the **Universal Necessity of their (balanced) division and union for the actualization/continuation of Life?** Let us see.

Franz Hartmann, M.D. (1838-1912)—*The Life of Jehoshua, The Prophet of Nazareth,* 1888

"The *Cross* has a far deeper signification; it is a symbol that was known thousands of years before the advent of modern Christianity; it may be found in Indian cave-temples and upon relics dating from antediluvian times. It cannot mean the death of a god, for gods are immortal and cannot be killed; it means the entire cessation of all thoughts of self—of all self-love, self-will; it means the *mystic death,* the renunciation of everything belonging to personality and limitation, and the entering in a life in the Infinite, Unlimited, and Eternal."

"But Jehoshua spoke of a heavenly state, where no one is married nor given in marriage; where there is no distinction of sex or race or of religious opinion; where each individual soul is a spiritual power, a note in the great symphony that constitutes the harmony of the All; a state in which we will all be *one in Divinity,* as we are now *one in Humanity;* an existence where all are cemented together by the universal principle of Love, where individual consciousness is swallowed up in the inconceivable happiness of eternal and universal existence, of which men cannot conceive intellectually as long as they cling to form, and which is therefore like nothing to them."

"Even the Pharisees of the world and the reasoning powers in Man are willing to listen to the voice of the truth as long as it does not come in conflict with their selfish interests. All men admire the truth, as long as he remains in his cage and does not threaten their self-interest; but when he overthrows a favourite creed, then will they drive him away from the city. Then will the spirit of Wisdom have to retire to some quiet place, to wait until the storm of the passion has ceased, when it may again attempt to enter the heart."

In the first passage he speaks of: "...*it means the entire cessation of all thoughts of self—of all self-love, self-will; it means the mystic death, the renunciation of everything belonging to personality and limitation, and the entering in a life in the Infinite, Unlimited, and Eternal."* Let me ask, does *mystic death* mean we don't even have a sense of our individual selves? How is that going to work? We can only touch another, and be touched by another, from our individual selves. Self-consciousness is a requirement of consciousness, as is a consciousness of the Other. There is both the division and the unification, not just the unification. We all have self-interest. And, note, part of that self-interest is an interest in another. Why? Because we do not and cannot create by ourselves alone. Everything, if you will, is a procreation, and all procreation takes an equal and opposite two.

In the second passage we see: *"...But Jehoshua spoke of a heavenly state, where no one is married nor given in marriage; where there is no distinction of sex or race or of religious opinion;... a state in which we will all be one in Divinity, as we are now one in Humanity; an existence where all are cemented together by the universal principle of Love, where individual consciousness is swallowed up in the inconceivable happiness of eternal and universal existence of which men cannot conceive intellectually as long as they cling to form, and which is therefore like nothing to them."* Can you see the **One Force Misconception** in play here? This is the issue of Life as to non-Life. There isn't any Life in a "One Force Misconception." **Life is a Two-Force Sexual (Equal and Opposite) Giving-Receiving Interchange between the Two Forces of Male and Female.** Balance/Life does not arise from singularity or some zero comprehension/consciousness of Self. Balance/Life comes from the Equal and Opposite awareness of the equal necessity of Man (Division) and Woman (Unification). Do you see the distinction? **Man and Woman (Equal and Opposite) Balance Equals Life!***

* For a review of the radioactive holocaust we are facing due to our spiritual, mental, and physical imbalances see the book *Atomic Suicide?* by Walter and Lao Russell, 1957. I am using the term radioactive to include any thought/action that moves us to destruction.

Now let's review the third passage along with a passage from *Witness* by Whitter Chambers. I will separate these passages out.

Franz Hartmann, M.D. (1838-1912)—*The Life of Jehoshua, The Prophet of Nazareth*, 1888

"Even the Pharisees of the world and the reasoning powers in Man are willing to listen to the voice of the truth as long as it does not come in conflict with their selfish interests. All men admire the truth, as long as he remains in his cage and does not threaten their self-interest; but when he overthrows a favourite creed, then will they drive him away from the city. Then will the spirit of Wisdom have to retire to some quiet place, to wait until the storm of the passion has ceased, when it may again attempt to enter the heart."

Whittaker Chambers (1901-1961)—*Witness*, 1952

"I am a man who, reluctantly, grudgingly step by step, is destroying himself that this country and the faith by which it lives may continue to exist."

I, too, am that man. I am a man who, reluctantly, grudgingly step-by-step, is destroying himself that this universe and the faith (in Man and Woman Balance by which it not yet knows it lives) may continue to exist.

photo 2004

"The measure of your love is dependent not on what you believe nor on the size of your 'giving' but on the purity of your heart."

Etheric Materialization Into Form is nothing more or less then the Procreant Process of Life given to us through the two eternal (equal and opposite) forces of Male and Female, i.e., all creativity is actually a procreativity.

Etheric Materialization Into Form

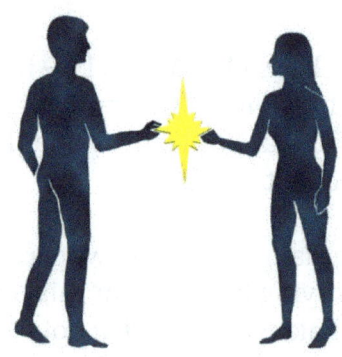

If I may, I will now bid you all farewell. My purpose (**To bring the message of Man and Woman Balance to planet Earth**) is now complete. May I leave you with one last poem from the writing **To Cassandra—Early Years © 1985, 1994**

Sometimes It Hurts To Be A Poet

Sometimes it hurts
To be a poet
Inside,
Yes, it hurts inside
For the old poet knows
That he must stand aside
Be apart
From all the heartfelt cheers
The tender moments of love
Or the agony of life's fears
If he is to ever feel

Just how it must be
To stand in that other's shoes
To look through that other's eyes
And see off in the distance
An old poet
Standing so very much by himself
Alone.

Addendum: Author Presentations

A note from the author

The following presentations were written during the years of 2006 – 2007. I had at one time envisioned doing a series of workshops. Little did I know what I personally and mankind in general had yet to go through. I wonder why we, men and women, will not seem to spiritually move one inch forward without first feeling great hardship.

I had forgotten about these presentations. There were "hidden" in one of my files on my computer. Just by luck I guess that I happened to run across them. I don't know that they will enhance your understanding or appreciation of this writing. But, for me, I wanted to make them available; not that at this time I want to do workshops. I just want to make them available. I think the writing is beautiful and may touch your soul in some new way.

Christopher Alan Anderson

January 19, 2025

Author Presentations

The following are topics the author is available to speak on to groups desiring to learn and experience the depths of the message of Man and Woman Balance.

-But Do You Want Love?
-A Meditation Intensive on Sorting Out Relationships
-A Living Prayer for Relationship
-The Secret
-The Eternal Connection
-Winning As a Way of Life
-The Word
-Let There Be Light
-On Unalienable Rights
-The Illumination Called Romance
-The One Constant of the Universe
-Healing the Soul Forever
-The Procreant Nature of (Sexual) Surrender
-World Peace Through Man and Woman Balance
-Marriage: The Only Purpose of the Universe
-The Inwardness of Light
-The 1st Principle and Cognition
-The First Pair
-The Path

Copyright © 2007 Christopher Alan Anderson
Website: www.manandwomanbalance.com

But Do You Want Love?

For if you want anything, you must first have love. If you have love, you will have everything. If you don't have love, nothing will be yours. But do you want love?

Love is never possessed by oneself alone. It is shared equally, expressed as it is given and received. Love is not a belief to hold onto. Love is not an ideal to measure up to. Love is not a vision to compel the greater good. Love is simply a touch between two souls. But do you want love?

Love comes as it is given. As it is given, it again reappears to be re-given. Love is as a child, given birth to out of the recesses of two trembling hearts, a man and a woman clutching each other through their one pure touch in each and every moment, right now. But do you want love?

A Meditation Intensive
On
Sorting out Relationships

...constitutes a shift into an eternal world of eternal love, one always with his or her other.

What is relationship—its archetype in the world? In this 1-day intensive, this is the question we ask. Our purpose here is to get down to the one original pattern or model (of relationship) from which all things adhere throughout the universe. Upon doing so you will come into a perfect balance—*healing*—with the most primordial relationship of your life, which will then extend to every relationship in your life.

Handouts

The Legend of the Truth
Let Us Create Life Together
The Light at the End of the Mind
Romance—How to Find It and Keep It
The Birthing Process
Aphorisms for the New Age of Man and Woman
Please Believe in Us
Initiation into Eternal Life
The Faith That Moves Mountains
The Marriage Vow

A Living Prayer for Relationship

Many of us today find ourselves missing the one thing we really want—*a relationship.* How may we bring forth that relationship we truly desire and have felt is just around the corner since time immemorial? Could it be that we have forgotten how to pray? This is not to suggest a religion or ideology but a method of prayer that will connect you to that special other that you have always felt to be residing in your heart. In this workshop, we will actually learn how to make *A Living Prayer for Relationship* upon which *when spoken* will bring you and your only begotten together.

This workshop is not just for singles but for couples as well. Many couples still feel a gap or separation in their relationship not knowing how to close it. *A Living Prayer for Relationship* works for both singles and couples who feel a distance in their relationship be it physical, emotional, financial, common interest, purposive, parental, or spiritual. The *Living Prayer for Relationship* process is universal to every man and woman. Whatever state or condition you find yourself to be in regarding relationship, come join us for this once in a lifetime opportunity to discover *The Living Prayer for Relationship* for yourself, realizing once and for all that you are never alone.

The Secret

...to life, love, success, riches, good fortune, romance, health, happiness, purpose, beauty, grace, confidence, clarity, energy sufficiency, environmental integrity, world peace, political and economic stability, parent and child harmony, critical education, joy, trust ...

...to manifestation, creation, wisdom, inspiration, balance, attunement, abundance, well-being, spiritual perfection, eternal connection, universal intelligence, cognitive telepathy, cosmic identity, primary synchronization, the control of the cause behind all effect...

The *Secret* has been sought for throughout the ages by philosophers, metaphysicians, prophets, poets, mystics, spiritual seers, shamans, religious leaders, psychologists, politicians, legislators, scholars in all fields, educators, scientists, artists, psychics, healers, meditators, and men and women in every walk of life.

The *Secret* has never been known. Irrespective of all the promises, it still remains hidden—part of the great mystery. Is it that the light is just too bright? Perhaps it is because we already think we know what it is. Whatever the case, the *Secret* is now available to all those interested in sharing in its light.

The Eternal Connection

In this day of searching for our perfect or higher self or higher or spiritual power, etc., one thing remains certain, we will not establish the connection to the eternal that we seek. The desire for an eternal connection resides within each man and woman as the core of their purpose, perfection, and fulfillment in life. The essence of philosophy, religion, spirituality, psychology, and any new age quest are all based in establishing this one connection. We must kneel at the throne of some higher power we are told or, conversely, go within ourselves, i.e., "be still and know," or come to experience the "oneness" supposedly lying beneath all experience. And on it goes--another "teacher" shows up just in time to support us in climbing to the top of the mountain, neither of us realizing we have just made the trek to the top of the wrong mountain once again.

The Eternal Connection is a one-day meditation intensive in making certain distinctions so that we can climb the right mountain and thereby connect with the eternal. The answer lies not in faith, feelings, experience, psychic or spiritual knowing, or even in enlightenment/illumination but in a simple (2 + 2 = 4) understanding that opens the door for us to actually and concretely know—for the first time—what the eternal is and what it is not. Please join us on the trek of a lifetime, all the way to the top of the right mountain. And, yes, there is a right as to wrong mountain.

Winning
As a Way of Life

Tired of being a loser? Me, too. And it's not easy, is it? It seems that the forces of irrationality have us by the hairs. Or is it just one giant big conspiracy—a matrix that controls us that we cannot identify? Or perhaps, even more to the point, there is something within ourselves, a misunderstanding or mis-premise, that actually ensures our continued loser status? Whatever the case may be, in this one-day Meditation Intensive, we will identify *exactly* the block that prevents us all from being a winner in life. *"All win, all the time"*—that shall be our motto.

The idea of winning as a way of life ought not to be considered a pop psychology, the latest feel-good promotion, or some positive thinking/visualization method. Winning actually is encoded in life as life. Each of us is born to win. Losing is not an option. It's not about faith per se. Rather, it is about metaphysical law. In metaphysical law, losing is the great illusion. Winning, in everything we do, is our only option. *"All win, all the time"*—that shall be our *reality*.

Let us join together in this most wonderful inquiry on winning. The winner's circle awaits us one last time.

The Word

In the beginning was *the word* and *the word* was _____. What do we put into that space? Do we put the word *God* or *Yahweh* in there? Perhaps we should put *I AM* or *I AM That I AM* in that place. Maybe we should put some word like light or energy or spirit or mind or love—something, an ether or Tao or First Principle. Whatever is the "what is," certainly that should be *the word,* shouldn't it? The truth of the matter is that we do not know what *the word* is. If we did we would know why *the word* is *the word* and, furthermore, why no other word can suffice as *the word*. Imagine, all this time, all this talk, and we still do not know.

But what if we did know? What if we could know—can you imagine the power we would have (not over others) to actually live rightly? In one moment, everything would change. We could live in harmony with things; we could truly love our neighbor as ourselves; we could align with the creative forces and solve our problems—energy, poverty, war, and sickness, to name a few, if only we knew what *the word* was. In this one-day workshop that is what you will come to know. When you leave you will know what *the word* is and why *the word* is *the word* and, in fact, could not be anything else but *the word*. And, in that moment, everything will change. And, more importantly, you will know what to do. Please come join us in this most greatest of opportunities—the discovery of *the word.*

Let There Be Light

The declaration and/or command *Let There Be Light* arises from the beginning of time. Of all the commands, this may be the greatest. Yet, what does it actually mean? From where does it originate—within our souls? How may we incorporate it into our lives so that we may equally stand upon the stars and declare for all time, *Let There Be Light.*

The above questions are just a few of the questions we will reflect upon in this one-day Meditation Intensive. At the heart of all these questions arises the one elementary question, *what is light?* If we were to ask that question of ourselves the common reply might be *luminosity*. But can we delve deeper into ourselves and discover the source of luminosity?

In New Age parlance we often hear the term, *the light.* One might even declare, *"I am the light."* And so we try but the light still does not shine. Being "the light," as it were, does not guarantee or command the light to shine. Again, we must go deeper.

This Meditation Intensive is for those who have room in their souls for one more step—*into the light.* Come join us in the most unusual inquiry on bringing the light into the understanding such that we may illuminate the world from our command—*Let There Be Light.*

On Unalienable Rights
Why We Never Had Them

...that they are endowed with certain unalienable rights... Who can forget that phrase in the most famous document on freedom ever penned by the hand of man—*The Declaration of Independence*? And yet, everywhere we turn we seem to be bogged down by the licensing board, the regulatory agency, the taxation bureaucracy, laws that go against common sense and economic hope, politicians that set their own perks and pensions, the tidal wave of the demand for more entitlements as if somehow an entitlement was an unalienable right. Could it be that in the history of the world we have never really had *unalienable* rights? And could the reason that we have never really had unalienable rights be because we actually have never known what they really are? How many of us can define the nature and origin of an unalienable right? How many of us want to?

In this one-day workshop we will do just that—*define the nature and origin of unalienable rights.* The reason for this is that we are not really able to achieve our wants and desires in life without them. We struggle on against the forces of the borg only to be defeated once more. Isn't it time to clear the air and expose the conspiracy that has been keeping us in the dark for thousands of years, claiming that whatever rights are they certainly are not unalienable? Come join us in this most intriguing program that will allow you to understand and experience your eternal freedom via your *unalienable rights* once and for all.

The Illumination Called Romance

Romance is a special love that has come to be significant in relationships today. Most couples desire—and even demand—that <u>spark</u> of love that brings joy to their life together. The beauty about romance is that it can exist at every moment of a couples' relationship and, in doing so, give life to that relationship. But, the big question is, how? This question is answered in this 1-day workshop *The Illumination Called Romance.* What we, heretofore, have failed to understand is that romance is a light, a very special and beautiful light, that illuminates the souls of a man and a woman. In this workshop we will discover exactly what that light is and how to tap into it so that it may bath our own relationships in its beauty.

Many today would rather not think about such things as *the Illumination called Romance.* They want love to somehow just come to them, their feelings being their guide. Others might try and dominate their relationships without consideration for the spiritual significance of the other. And still others turn the whole thing over to some "higher power," failing to understand that the love must come from their own hearts. In short, we fail to see that romance is actually a very defined and exacting idea that takes a special effort to bring to consciousness. But that is a part of its joy, in knowing just how special it is and how wonderful it is when we can give it to our beloved without any circumstance ever able to interfere. Come join us in defining and sharing this most special light called romance and illuminate your relationship today.

The One Constant
Of The Universe

What is the one constant of the universe, that thing or process that you can depend on in every situation? No matter where you find yourself to be, in some alternative universe or reality where the rules appear to be different, in some situation you have yet to cognize, in some awake or dream state where the forces around you seem to be against you, there it is--*the one constant of the universe* ready to give coherence to your every thought and breath.

Is the one constant what we historically call "God" or "spirit" or the "witness" behind all thought and form? Maybe the one constant is whatever we each think it is, a subjective constant. Maybe it is some nature spirit or Gaia consciousness—if we could just experience our "oneness" together some shout. Maybe we should just explore the nature of the question and not look for answers. Or just maybe we should wait for our great leaders to tell us, our ministers and educators, our politicians and lawyers, our scientists and physicians, for certainly they always have our best in mind, don't they?

If you have arrived at a place in your life where you would like to just sweep all the old (beliefs and hopes) under the rug and begin anew, this workshop is certainly for you. In this workshop, you will have the opportunity to step beyond all that has come before and enter into the *one constant of the universe*. And from this moment on, it will never change. It will always be what it is for that is its nature. It cannot ever be anything but what it is. Are you ready to step forward into this level of accountability—for life?

Healing the Soul Forever

The center point of all healing lies in our souls. Our souls are our individual expressions of the living light of which there are various names. It is imperative then that our souls be healed so this living light can be expressed through us. Now, one may suggest that this living light or spiritual perfection already exists within us as us, so what is the problem? This actually may be the case. But until we know that <u>one unique balance point</u> between our light soul and another's, all the wishing, praying, exploring, or investigating will not right or heal us. This is especially true of today's New Age movement where everyone seems so sure they have found their own source or truth. The source or truth actually does not lie within us. It lies as a connective point between us. This is the difference.

In this workshop, we will have the opportunity to come to recognize and embrace this <u>one unique balance point</u>. In doing so we will come to the astonishing realization that our souls are not just healed, but that they are healed *forever*. From this <u>one unique balance point</u> we can never go back to the old days of confusion, angst, doubt, and suffering. No matter where and under what circumstances we may find ourselves in the future—from incarnated lives to new forms and visions—we will know and hold this balance.

If you have an interest in having your soul healed forever, please come join us in this one-day workshop that will allow you to glow—from this moment on--from the inside out.

The Procreant Nature
Of (Sexual) Surrender

As per our spiritual evolution, we are moving into an age where we seek our purpose, meaning, value, ecstasy, and even transcendence in the sexual domain. The significance of Freud was in the demarcation point that we, in our essence, are not just beings (or even spiritual beings) but, first and foremost, we are sexual beings. We live sexual lives. We don't just live as some type of unisex minds or spirits through sexual bodies, rather our bodies, minds, and spirits are <u>sexual in nature</u>, which is to say--*The nature of a thing lies in its sexuality, male or female.* And so <u>relationship</u> moves to the forefront of our lives and rightly so.

Having said this it is quite obvious to notice that something very essential is being left out of the conversation on sexual surrender or sexual union—the new proof of enlightenment as it were! It is not enough to understand the sexual nature of things or even the innate differences between men and women, critical as that is. We must also understand that centering this most essential relationship is the <u>procreant</u>. *The nature of all sexual surrender/union is procreant.* We seek this surrender/union to procreate, not just physically but mentally and spiritually as well. In any surrender/union, the child cannot be left out of consciousness. The child is always calling to be born. A surrender or union will not be complete if the child is not heard. It is in the child, the procreant nature of the universe, that surrender/union truly occurs.

In this workshop, we will look to find that placement in our hearts where not only our sexual other half resides but also that child that will be born out of our unity together. When that placement is found spiritual beauty or radiance is (re)produced once more.

World Peace Through Man and Woman Balance

Oh, the cry for world peace, if only we could have peace amongst ourselves. If only we could bring all conflict to a close. Mustn't we do our duty and attend another peace rally (power to the people), have another peace day and worship our "oneness" together? Yes, let us get serious and "demand" peace. "We <u>demand</u> peace," the crowd shouts. "We demand peace <u>now</u>." Yet the conflict continues for, you see, no one really asks the mostly unconsciousness question—what is the root of the conflict? Where does the war wage in our own souls? Might we consider the possibility that the conflict lies in the imbalance we currently hold <u>right now</u> with our own eternal other half, that equal but opposite of ourselves who is always with each one of us? Let us consider that the only conflict in this world is the one each one of us is having right now with our equal and opposite eternal other half? Could it be, that if we could somehow balance this <u>one singular relationship</u> that all conflict would disappear from the face of this planet? If so, we must ask ourselves, do we really want conflict to disappear, or is that just some more hot air?

In this workshop, we will look to balance this one singular relationship of our lives and, by so doing, bring true and everlasting peace into this world. This stand or declaration will not be more hot air for it will come from the <u>balance</u> that exists at each moment between a man and a woman that is the definition of life itself. To choose life is to choose peace. It cannot be done any other way. Please join us in an unrelenting stand for peace that is founded on the balance of life.

Marriage
The Only Purpose of the Universe

What the universe actually is, its construct and its purpose, has always been a great mystery. That the universe would even have an order much less a purpose in its being is somewhat mind boggling. And yet, as we contemplate this grandeur, one thing appears certain—there is <u>life</u>. There is life in this universe and at the center of this life process is the <u>procreant</u>—that union/division between sexual opposites that is the rebirth and lineage of life everlasting. And so one can only ask, what might be that one absolutely necessary ingredient that supports the procreant nature of life? The answer is <u>marriage</u>. Marriage—a simple couple of words, *I DO,* spoken by a man and a woman, out of the recognition of the necessity to make a commitment to each other so that the life of a child can be given the love—*their love*—that is so absolutely necessary for that child to survive. In here, we see that marriage is the gatekeeper of survival—survival being an absolute necessity for life.

In this day and age of so much confusion in relationships not to mention an inability to commit to another in marriage by holding to those magic words *I DO* in any circumstance, we all need to reconnect to the importance of marriage as the only purpose of the universe. This is not a mandate to you but an opportunity to meet the grandeur that resides within you so you can again give to your most special other the stance of life. Please come join us in this magical workshop and experience the center of the universe—*marriage*—to be of your own eternal giving.

The Inwardness of Light

Far too often, when dealing with the subject of illumination, the experience is misinterpreted. The light that truly shines does not come to one but from one. It, in its nature, exists inwardly. And yet, too often, people think they "know." It's just assumed actually. That "knowing" might be something they were taught or read or have come to through a spiritual discipline or just from the course of life. Whatever the case, that "knowing," more often than not, resides as an external placement within them. It doesn't speak from the deepest recesses of the universe. It doesn't hold all power in its form. It lacks certain credibility even if the applause is great. The naked purity of heart along with the strength of carrying the humility of truth is missing. Ah, but how does one get to this most essential placement in the inward world of light?

In this workshop our task will be to wade into that inward location where the light is revealed in all its glory. We will do so by a most interesting method--actually clarifying our languaging via defining our terms. It is often said that the true light or reality of life cannot be defined and/or expressed, only experienced. Let us rather say, *if we are unable to define/language the nature of a something then let us stop at that point and make no further claims.* What is not or cannot be defined and/or expressed has no concern for us as conscious beings.

If you are ready to look at the most direct and clear light in this universe then please join us for this most illuminating of programs. The light is what it is. In being what it is, it can be defined. In being defined it can be brought to consciousness. In being brought to consciousness, it can be experienced and shared one to another.

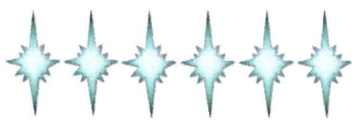

The 1st Principle and Cognition

"If I could just get what I want, then I would be happy." How many of us have said those words in some form or another? I know I have. Yet, the underlying issue here is one of manifestation. How do we manifest those deepest desires of our heart that we have held onto for so long? The key lies in our cognition (knowing) of the 1st principle of all things. This is to say that we must cognize or bring to consciousness the 1st principle from which we can then place our specific desire into. It is not enough to believe or pray or have faith. It is not enough to do good works or be in service or be creative in some way. We actually must be conscious of the 1st principle—the why of it. From there we just take our desire and drop it into its center. What this does is anchor our individual desire as one with the universal process of life. Once our individual desire is anchored in this fashion, there isn't any choice but that it will manifest.

The reason why so many people cannot seem to manifest their desires is because they drop them into a "center" that is not the 1st principle. For example, let's say you place your desire on the "saving grace" of Christianity, or the "oneness experience" of I AM, or the "thought is creative" New Thought movement or the "I create my own reality" New Age movement, etc., and wonder why your desire does not manifest. It is because you have placed your desire into something that is not the 1st principle. It cannot manifest for it is out of alignment with the 1st principle. Correct the alignment and the manifestation will then occur. So the question before us then is, <u>what is the 1st principle</u>?

In this discussion, we will cognize the 1st principle into our minds from which we then place our desires into and watch the manifestation begin.

The First Pair

If we were asked what the First Pair is, that is to say, what that idea means to us, probably most of us would answer something along the lines of "the story of creation via Adam and Eve." But I wonder how often we actually look into the meaning and importance of the idea of a First Pair. Let me just ask some basic questions that come to my mind. What is the meaning, both in metaphysical and practical terms, of a First Pair? Who really was or is the First Pair and how would we even answer that question? Is the First Pair sexual, i.e., male and female, and, if so, why? Was the First Pair created by something else or does creation actually come out of the First Pair, and, if that is the case, what would be that process? Does the idea of a First Pair help or hinder us in understanding the truth of life and our own unique purposes in life? I am sure there are many other questions one could come up with but in just looking at the few I have asked, I think it is safe to say that the idea of a First Pair presents us with a great deal to ponder.

In this workshop, we will bring to the table the above questions and any others we can ask concerning the idea of a First Pair. And moreover, we will see how the idea of a First Pair actually can give to us the structure to answer any questions we may have. (We don't need to be continuously stuck in the question!) In other words, it just may be this idea of a First Pair that brings order out of the chaos once and for all. That in itself would be a glorious thing. Please come join with us in the discovery of the First Pair and actually find yourself, "who you are," for the first time.

The Path

It is often said that there are many paths to the truth. One might even surmise that each one of us has our own path, and, in walking our own unique path, will eventually arrive. After all, aren't our religions themselves but just different paths to the truth? But wait, did not Jesus himself state in John 14:6: *"I am the way and the truth and the life. No one comes to the Father except through me."* Here is a man (certainly the leader of one of the great religions) who doesn't just suggest but states that there is only one path—*"except through me."* Now, I am not making this point to advocate Christianity; I suggest a different path. But I am making this point to suggest that there is only one path to the truth. Let me further claim that unless one is coming from this *one path*, he or she will never get to the truth. And so it appears that the path one chooses is critically important as to whether or not one ever arrives.

In this workshop, we will be looking at the underlying premises that make up one's path to see if those premises have any alignment to *life*. In short, if our path is not aligned upon the *truth of life* going in, we can never get to a *life of truth* going out. This is to say, *the discovery of the correct path is the discovery of the truth itself.* Who would have thought? Join us, if you will, in the discovery of the *one* path that takes each one of us to the *truth* simply because it is the *truth*.

Author: Christopher Alan Anderson (1950-) received the basis of his education from the University of Science and Philosophy, Swannanoa, Waynesboro, Virginia. He resides in the transcendental/romantic tradition, that vein of spiritual creativity of the philosopher and poet. His quest has been to define and express an eternal *romantic* reality from which a man and a woman could *together* stand and create a *living* universe. Mr. Anderson began these writings in 1971. The first writings were published in 1985.

photo 2004

Writings by the Author:
The Divine Touch: A New Creation for Life!
Humanitarian Project: Man and Woman Balance
Etheric Materialization Into Form!
Selected Writings—Volume 3: A New Trinity
Channeling the Eternal Woman
The Case Against Man and Woman – A Philosophy on Trial
Meditations for Deepening Love
Let There Be Life!
Meditation as Spiritual Procreation
Spiritual Healing of Our Eternal Souls for All Time
The Man and Woman Manifesto: What We Believe!
The Prime Movers: The Sovereigncy of Man and Woman
Reflections on Light: From a Homeless Shelter
The Metaphysics of Sex …in a Changing World!
Wealth Plus+ Empowering Your Everyday!
To Cassandra—Early Years

The 2008 - 2009 Articles
Man, Woman, and God
The Man and Woman Relationship: A New Center for the Universe
Illumination
Selected Writings—Volume 2
The Discovery of Life
The Man and Woman Manifesto: Let the Revolution Begin
Psychotherapy As If Life Really Mattered
The Universal Religion: The Final Destiny of Mankind
The Truth Revealed: My Answer to the World
Healing In The Light & The Art and Practice of Creativity
Selected Writings

For ordering information go to: www.manandwomanbalance.com

"Bringing Man and Woman Together!"

www.ingramcontent.com/pod-product-compliance
Lightning Source LLC
Chambersburg PA
CBHW071719090426
42738CB00009B/1822